I am Prodigal

Moving from SHAME to GRACE

David R. Stokes

I AM PRODIGAL: Moving from SHAME to GRACE

Copyright © 2017 David R. Stokes

Critical Mass Books
Fairfax, Virginia
www.criticalmassbooks.com

ISBN-10: 1-947153-02-1
ISBN-13: 978-1-947153-02-8

All scripture references in this book, unless otherwise indicated, are from the New International Version (copyright © 1973, 1978, 1984 by International Bible Society). When other translations are cited, the following initials are used: KJV (King James Version), NKJV (New King James Version), and NLT (New Living Translation).

Cover Design: Eowyn Riggins
Layout: Penoaks Publishing, http://penoaks.com

Visit the author's website: www.davidrstokes.com

Special discounts are available on quantity purchases by churches and group ministries. For details visit: www.expectationbooks.com.

To all who have strayed and all who have stayed.
Please come home.

Contents

Foreword

"Prone to wander, Lord I feel it,
Prone to leave the God I love."

I am reminded of these timeless lyrics as Pastor David Stokes (or simply Pastor, as I get to call him) describes our common struggle in his latest book: *I Am Prodigal: Moving from Shame to Grace.*

Sometimes we are the wandering squanderer son, selfishly looking for greener pastures. Sometimes we are the self-righteous brother crying "woe is me," when we see someone getting the attention we desire. Or maybe, we find ourselves in the father's shoes, when he sadly must let go, so the son can fully understand the truth that fulfillment isn't found in the bright lights of a party, or at the bottom of a bottle, but in living close to the Father—the Heavenly Father.

Life takes us down many roads, and for some of us, those roads lead far away. But as Pastor Stokes delves deep into Jesus' familiar parable, it's clear that God wants us to realize that he understands our nature and our—even those that take us away from His heart.

He knows how impulsive we can be. He knows how pious and stubborn we can be. And he shows us that the Father loves us endlessly through it all. He chases after us, wanting us to come home.

As Pastor Stokes puts it so well, we can either let conviction and repentance lead us to *grace*, or let guilt and pride lead us to the *grave*. It's our choice.

#IAmProdigal

Rev. Lucas Johnson
Connections Pastor
Expectation Church
December 2017

CHAPTER ONE

The Prodigal Pathology

The British novelist Charles Dickens (1812-1870), famous for many works including *A Tale of Two Cities,* once remarked about a short story that could be titled *A Tale of Two Sons,* the story of the *Prodigal Son,* that it was the greatest short story in history. Mark Twain agreed.

So do I.

Though it's only about 500 words long depending on the translation, it's filled with powerful imagery about love, family, home, God, us, rebellion, redemption, righteousness, self-righteousness, joy, sorrow, sin, salvation, confession, and so much more.

As you read these words, you may be tempted to think, "Been there, done that," but I urge you resist the notion that because the elements and scenes of this epic story are familiar, we have exhausted its value to us.

We haven't.

We're going to explore every word in this story—and then the words behind the words. Please don't let familiarity breed indifference. The nuances in this story will be of great benefit to everyone, from the scriptural novice to the advanced student of the Bible.

A few years ago, we adopted as our mission statement at Expectation Church in Fairfax, Virginia: "To bring those who are far from God to experience faith in Christ." It's simply a reflection of the heart of Jesus, who "came to seek and to save what was lost."[1] The entire Gospel of Luke seems to have this particular interest, pointing us to story after story of Jesus and his affinity for outcasts and lost causes.

This story, if understood correctly, should make us uncomfortable and challenge some of our "religious" assumptions. For example, it's quite easy to think of this as a great story for "the other guy"—someone we know who has really messed up. But there is code in this parable, code that indicates an all-too-common pattern that may hit closer to home.

This parable has its root in ancient prophecy; something recorded several hundred years before the birth of Jesus and his whirlwind ministry. The prophecy was uttered by a man named Isaiah and includes a few sentences—a biblical verse—that captures the essence of God's heart and purpose in a manner similar to the famous passage John 3:16.

"We all, like sheep, have gone astray, each of us has turned to his own way, and the Lord has laid on him the iniquity of us all."[2]

It's one of the greatest *messianic* verses in all of sacred scripture. It forecasts the ultimate sacrifice of Christ on the cross, and it highlights the reason for it—human beings have a tendency to wander away from God.

There's a venerable hymn that dates back to the days of The Great Awakening in America—decades before the Declaration of Independence, written by a minister named Robert Robinson. As a young man, he encountered the powerful preaching of George Whitefield—the voice of the revival sweeping across the colonies. He was converted and soon was a preacher himself. He eventually penned the words of a hymn that expressed the joy of his faith in Christ, its lines saturated with praise to God. But in the final stanza, Robinson added some haunting words— haunting but honest. Even in his joy, he knew that there was part of him—a tendency in his heart—that reminded him that he was still a sinner, even though he had been saved by grace:

> *Prone to wander, Lord, I feel it,*
> *Prone to leave the God I love*
> *Take my heart, O take and seal it*
> *Seal it for thy courts above.*[3]

Robinson's words are a sometimes painful reminder that we all have what we might call a *prodigal gene*, a propensity for wandering—for going astray. Facing this fact, and being honest about it, is very important. So as we begin the journey through these pages, I want to start with a caveat. It's very tempting to use the story of the Prodigal Son (or any biblical text, for that matter) as a prism through which to view and critique *others*.

That's a mistake.

If we really understand what Jesus was saying, we need to be comfortable, or at least honest, enough with ourselves to realize that we are all prodigals.

I am prodigal.

We all are.

The only mention of this particular parable is found in Luke's gospel. This writer also penned The Acts of the Apostles. He was a physician and a faithful companion of the Apostle Paul. We don't know much about his personal life from scripture, but we can surmise that he was strongly influenced by Greek philosophy and culture.

Personally, I think he was a Gentile, which would make him the only non-Jewish writer in the New Testament. I'm not dogmatic about this, but it does seem to explain his unique *voice*, one that highlighted Jesus' ministry to those on the fringe of society—*outcasts* and *outsiders*.

The story of the man with two sons must be seen in context. Luke describes the story as one of three—all flowing from an encounter with three components of an audience listening to Christ's teaching.

"Now the tax collectors and sinners were all gathering to hear him. But the Pharisees and the teachers of the law muttered, 'This man welcomes sinners and eats with them.'"

We see three groups. There were tax collectors. These were also called in the old English, *publicans.* Not Republicans, but publicans. *Publicans* were Jewish people who were basically in cahoots with the Roman occupiers. They purchased franchises to collect taxes, but they had broad discretion to pressure people about those taxes. And they worked on commission, so the more they collected, the more they pocketed. They were often the wealthiest people in town, but they were scorned. They were outcasts. They were hated. They were traitors, sort of the up-and-outers. They were like gangsters. They lived well, but it was at the expense of their fellow-citizens.

Not cool.

Then there were those simply called *sinners*. These were the prostitutes, drunks, addicts, thieves, and other criminals. They gathered to hear Jesus. He had this message that drew them in—in fact, they felt welcomed and comfortable around him.

Finally, some Pharisees were there—the chronic critics who made it their job to try to torment Jesus and harass anyone who wanted to hear what he had to say. Actually, the Pharisees didn't start out several hundred years earlier to be the bad guys. They were very interested in preserving and defending biblical truth. Not a bad thing. But along the way, pride crept in and their passion for truth morphed into pride-driven prejudice. They were poster-children for self-righteousness.

They saw the interaction between Jesus and the outcasts as scandalous and outrageous. The fact that they were comfortable with Jesus, and he with them, was contrary to everything they stood for. The very word "Pharisee" literally meant "one who separates." They believed that any contact with undesirable people led to potential contamination. They saw Jesus as a rogue rabbi, a teacher who attracted the wrong kind of people.

Years later, long after the crucifixion, resurrection, birth of the church, and the beginning of apostolic ministry, followers of Jesus began to hear a particular insult from the residents of the Syrian city of Antioch. They heard the word "Christian." It was meant as a criticism, at first. Popular culture rejected Jesus Christ, so the people extended it to those who wanted to be like him. However, believers decided to wear it as a badge of honor.

In the middle of the eighteenth century, two brothers studying at the University of Oxford—John and Charles Wesley—formed a club with a few other like-minded young men. Their purpose was to encourage each other in faith and holy living. In fact, they chose to call it the "Holy Club." But other students mocked them and their efforts. Noting that the Christian men were very particular about how they lived and conducted themselves—their "methods" being exact and meticulous—they began to mock them with the nickname, "methodists." The "Holy Club" turned it around and adopted the name.

I think about this when I read about how some criticized Jesus for his close encounters with sinners. Of course, he was the friend of sinners.

He still is.

As an aside, having grown up around church all my life, I wonder how often the body language of God's people has been more like that of the Pharisees than the Lord himself? We must move beyond "seeker friendly" toward "sinner friendly."

For the benefit of the publicans, the sinners, and the Pharisees (three audiences), Jesus told three stories. The first two—one about a lost coin and another about a lost sheep—built toward the third, which is the most famous of the trilogy—the story of the lost son. They were all illustrations of God's love for people. They're all about being lost and found.

There are two primary interpretive ways to apply these parables. They're pictures of God and lost humanity. We were created in innocence and surrounded by the beauty of Eden, but we fell into sin and lost it all. Yet God wants to reconcile and restore lost people. That's what salvation is. People are lost. They need to be found. It's a picture of salvation.

But, it was also a story about broken fellowship. There was a father and there were sons, and we know (if we know our Bible), that close relationship, not just of creator and created, but of father and child, is something we enter into by faith.

"Yet to all who received him, to those who believed in his name, he gave the right to become children of God."[5]

This popular notion of "the fatherhood of God and the brotherhood of man" is not a biblical construct. There is a sense that we are all connected to each other, of course, but sonship and the privileges of inheriting all spiritual blessings flow from a deliberately cultivated relationship—something we experience by faith. We're not automatically children of God by virtue of human birth, only via the new birth.[6]

I'm the son of Gerald Stokes. We have a genetic connection that binds us together biologically. But we also have a personal relationship—call it fellowship. As with any

7

human relationship, there are moments of closeness and even occasional moments of stress. Sometimes, parents and children can become estranged.

The picture of the father and the sons in Jesus' story is therefore also a picture of a person who is a believer, who experiences all the good things in the house of God, but who for whatever reason, makes choices contrary to what the Father wants. The parable is a message that says, "Hey, if you're not saved, you need to get saved." But, it's also a message that says, "If you've wandered away, please come home!"

We all have prodigal tendencies. I am prodigal. So are you. How can we find our way back home?

The story begins.

There was a man who had two sons. The younger one said to his father, 'Father, give me my share of the estate.' So he divided his property between them."

Just a few simple, yet powerful, facts. We'll assume there was no mother in the picture and that the sons were very important to the father's enterprise. Life was normal. Then one day—boom! The younger son made an outrageous request. The elements of the story are familiar. The younger son wandered off, things didn't work out, and he found his way back home. It's classic drama. Face it, we all are suckers for stories with happy endings—the good guy gets the girl, they all live happily ever-after, the wanderer returns.

It even works when the wanderer is a *dog*.

Growing up, one of my favorite movies was the 1943 feature, *Lassie Come Home*. It was the beginning of a long career on screens big and small for the indomitable female collie. Though Lassie was clearly the star of the film, there were a few other actors, like Roddy McDowall and even Elizabeth Taylor helping her.

But Lassie had a secret.

She was a *he*.

His name was *Pal*. He was a three-year-old long-haired collie. Pal was initially rejected for the role because, well, the part had been written for a female collie. Pal's owner brought him to a casting call for the movie and more than 1,500 dogs showed up. While Pal was rejected for the role that went to some silly girl dog, he was hired to do stunt work. Really. You can't make this stuff up. As the story goes, the film's producers decided to use recent flooding on the San Joaquin River for a few scenes involving the collie being swept away by the current and making it safely to dry ground. The female—a prize-winning show dog—wouldn't bite. Cue the canine double. Pal nailed the complicated scene in one "take," even selling it by laying down exhausted and perfectly still after extricating himself from the raging rapids.

A star was born.[8]

They even re-shot the first six-weeks of the movie with Pal. And in every Lassie story to come, in film or on television, you'd never hear anyone say, "Here, Lassie. Here, *boy*." Nope. It was always, "Good girl, Lassie." I wonder if Pal (who died in 1958, aged 18) ever tired of being called a girl? In the movie, Lassie got lost, experienced many challenges and dangers, but finally made it home. It's a story-telling formula that never fails.

And it all began with Jesus.

Why did the younger son in our Lord's story want to leave? Why do any of us feel prone to wander? Why do any of us tend to rebel against God? I can think of a few reasons.

Resentment

Maybe there was something about the life he had that he resented. He wouldn't be the first—or last—unhappy camper in a household. Resentment comes to us in many forms. We can get hurt by something. It can involve envy. There can be many triggers. We've all been there. But most people find ways to resolve those feelings. If not addressed or neutralized, resentment can burrow deep into our souls.

Every so often, news breaks about an earthquake somewhere in the world. Some are minor; others are major events leaving massive destruction in their wake. If you know anything about earthquakes or seismic activity, you know what happens on the surface is all tied to something that's happening well beneath the surface. They're commonly called *fault lines*. In other words, they're little fissures and breaks deep below the earth's crust. Such seismic activity can illustrate how great failures on the surface in our lives (read: public) often begin as secret "faults" deep in our hearts. Like resentment.

Possibly the younger son resented his *routine*.

Maybe he resented the *rules*.

He may have resented his *rank*.

We must always remember context when reading the Bible. In the Middle East at that time, being the firstborn was a big deal. It meant something called *birthright*. Being the firstborn now (I'm the oldest child of three) means absolutely nothing, except that you inherit more blame.

Likely, he resented his *role*.

His life was likely all planned out for him. He didn't have any choice in the matter. He and his big brother would follow in their father's footsteps and inherit the family business. This tradition was an important Middle Eastern value.

The seeds of the Prodigal's crop failure to come included resentment.

Restlessness

Maybe he was just bored and *restless*. People just get restless about things. Sometimes, that restlessness is fueled by *covetousness*. *"Thou shalt not covet..."* is the tenth commandment. Listen to the book of Hebrews. This is a great verse:

"Let your conduct be without covetousness; be content with such things as you have. For he himself has said, 'I will never leave you nor forsake you.'"[9]

That verse reminds us that in order to fully grasp the meaning of the word covetousness, we need to look at its polar opposite: *contentment*.

Let me describe it this way. Covetousness says, "I want *more*." Contentment says, "I have *enough*." So many choices in our lives involve the tension between those two states of mind.

By the way, it is not a mere cliché when that very same verse contains a reminder about God's promise to never leave us alone. Simply stated, the more conscious we are at any given moment of the presence of God, the more likely we are to come down on the side of being content with what we have. So, familiarity with God (in the sense of spiritual intimacy) breeds *contentment*.

Restlessness is also a form of ingratitude. When we lose sight of the connection between what we have in life and where it all comes from, we are on the slippery slope of unthankfulness. In my forty years as a pastor, I don't know how many times I've talked to people who've messed up their lives and they said something to this effect: "It took me a long time to realize how good I had it."

The cure for restlessness is *relentless gratitude*.

Romanticism

As with the younger son in the parable, the desire to wander off can be driven by *romanticism*. In other words, making the far country and everything out *there* look intriguing and attractive.

Henri Nouwen (1932-1996) was a Dutch Catholic priest and a prolific author. One day, while he was walking in a French village, he saw a poster of the famous portrait by Rembrandt, *The Return of the Prodigal Son*. He was awestruck and powerfully moved—so moved that he traveled in 1986 to Leningrad (now St. Petersburg) in the

Soviet Union to see the original on display at The Hermitage Museum. He spent several days staring at the painting and meditating on it. His thoughts were eventually put on paper and published in book form as *The Return of the Prodigal Son*. The volume is widely considered one of the most important Christian books of the twentieth-century. Among the countless gems of wisdom in its pages is this:

"I am the prodigal. I am the prodigal son every time I search for unconditional love where it cannot be found."[10]

The only place unconditional love, in the absolute sense, can be found is in God because we all fall short. There's never been a human being, other than Jesus, capable of complete, unconditional love. By the way, we all *want* unconditional love much more than we want to try to *express* unconditional love.

The Bible gives many examples of how people tend to romanticize things en route to making bad choices. Abraham and Lot have conflict and they're choosing where they're going to go. Abraham says, "You pick a direction. I'll go the other direction." Lot looks down toward the cities of Sodom and Gomorrah, cities notorious for their sin, the twin cities of evil and wickedness and vice. He sees the plains going toward them are well watered, and he describes them *"like the garden of the Lord."*[11] But in reality, it would prove to be anything but a garden spot. Romanticism drove Lot's directional choice and put him on the proverbial slippery slope.

Paul said to the Corinthians that even Satan himself can morph into something akin to an enlightened angel.[12] And he later warned young pastor Timothy about how attractive false things can be. *"Now the Spirit speaketh expressly, that in the latter times some shall depart from the faith, giving heed to seducing spirits, and doctrines of devils."*[13]

My point is, it's easy to romanticize things we all used to believe were wrong. You just look down the list of moral things, and now if you stand against them, you're the nut. Romanticism. Remember what the late humorist Erma Bombeck said? She titled one of her many books, *The Grass is Always Greener Over the Septic Tank*.

Oh yeah.

Repudiation

This is the final component of the prodigal pathology.

"The younger one said to his father, 'Father, give me my share of the estate.' So he divided his property between them."[14]

The decision was made to repudiate things that were part of the father's house. This is a curious verse because I've actually seen the father criticized here in some commentaries on this parable. But, I don't think you should criticize the father for enabling his son like this. Why? Because the father represents God in the story. In fact, you could call the parable, "The Prodigal Father" because the word *prodigal* doesn't mean rebellious; it means *wasteful* or *excessive* or *extravagant*. This is not just a story about the wastefulness and the excess of the son; it's also about the tremendous extravagance of the father's mercy and his grace.

Here's the lesson. God will always let us make the choice, even if it's the wrong choice.

The younger son's request would have certainly struck all those listening to Jesus that day as something completely outrageous because according to Middle Eastern customs, according to Jewish customs, there was something called law of *primogeniture*. Primogeniture dictated the rules of inheritance and the distribution of the father's estate.

Back then, when two brothers stood to inherit, the younger brother got one third, and the older brother received twice that. That's how it was done by law. That likely further fueled the resentment of the younger son. Remember, at that moment, the father didn't just give the inheritance to the younger son. He pulled himself out of the picture and gave *both* his sons their inheritance. So the older son, even though he would later be resentful, benefitted from his brother's repudiation of their father.

It would be like saying, "I wish you were dead. I want it to be like you're dead. Give me what comes to me," and the father divided to them his living. In the Greek language, the word *living*, often translated life, is a four-letter Greek word spelled in the English B-I-O-S. *Bios*. It is the root of the word biology which is about life, and biography, which is about an individual life. He's saying he divided among them his life, his living, everything he'd worked for.

Interestingly, the term *bios* came about early in the process of personal computers because there's an acronym B-I-O-S, which stands for *"Basic Input Operating System."* It's in your personal computer. It's essential to the function of that computer. Developers created that acronym. I can't find anywhere where they thought it'd be ironic to take the Greek word for life and put it here, but whether it was deliberate or it's just one of those interesting little ironies of language, the point is clear. The father was giving them the essence of the computer chip of his life, everything he'd worked for, everything he'd accumulated. It was all turned over to his sons. And the whole thing was a complete repudiation of everything the father had and had done.

I don't know how it happens. I don't know how someone goes from restlessness to repudiation, but I've seen it happen. I'm thinking of a case of someone I knew nearly twenty years ago. Good family. Good job. Successful. Beautiful home. Went to all the right Christian schools and colleges. Served in the church. Sang in the choir. Yet, about a year and a half ago, I got an email from this man. I hadn't seen him in years. He's renounced his faith. He's an atheist, and his mission in life now seems to be to tear down and destroy the faith of anybody who still believes. How does someone fall that far?

It happens when behavior begins to define belief, rather than letting *belief fuel behavior*.

The Psalm says, *"The fool has said in his heart, 'There is no God.'"* If you read the rest of the psalm (Psalm 53 and Psalm 14), it describes a pattern of moral corruption. When you encounter an alluring desire to behave in a way that's contrary to what you believe to be right, this creates mental and emotional tension that must somehow be resolved.

One way to resolve the tension is to reject the behavior. The other is to resolve it by redefining your values. That's what this man did. Lost his family. Lost his wife. Lost his career. Lost his faith. Instead of admitting he had lost all those things *because he had made moral choices that were destructive*, he blamed it on God and the fact he had had that faith in the first place. "If I hadn't had the faith I had, I'd be a happier man now," he said. No, you were blessed in the Father's house but you chose to repudiate it.

Now the great news. Spoiler alert. This is a story with a happy ending because the son does come home—the return of the prodigal. We're going to be exploring in depth the pathway, the journey, from shame to grace. *Guilt* is feeling bad about something you've done. *Shame* is feeling bad about who you are. One can be handled with confession and repentance. The other takes a while to realize you're valuable in the sight of God and that God loves you unconditionally, no matter what you've done or what you think you've done.

The shame, if not addressed, actually drives us back into more guilt and binds us more and more to sin and its collateral problems and damage.

Let me finish this chapter as I began. We go out where we came in. Do not say, "Well, I wish so-and-so would read this." We all need this. I am prodigal. So are you. We all, given the right (or better, wrong) circumstances, if we don't keep close to God and resolve things quickly before God, have the potential to the make a dangerous trip to a place far from God.

I have had prodigal moments in my life. Maybe they haven't been as extreme as in the parable, but the tendency has been there. I've not left everything behind, but there have been moments when I have been distant from God and just going through the motions. Then I heard the voice of the Holy Spirit calling, "Please come home. Please come home."

It doesn't matter to me whether you're just taking one step in the wrong direction or you've taken five, or if you've been going that way for a year or two or ten. You may even think, "There's no way back." Oh, yes, there is. You may feel like you've fallen under the ice and cannot find the hole to get back up through. But that fear ignores God's love and grace. Cry out to Him. God will melt every bit of ice on that surface with his grace and mercy so you can come up for the air of his love.

Please come home.

CHAPTER TWO

The Road to Ruin

The story of the prodigal son can be examined and applied in two primary ways. First, it's a picture of the great themes throughout Scripture—redemption and reconciliation; the idea that God created humanity and humanity has rebelled against him. Jesus came so he could pay the price for our sins, the penalty for sin, on the cross. It's a picture of salvation—a picture of a sinner who is coming home to have a relationship he's never had with the father he's never known.

It's also, however, a picture of someone who's already had a spiritual relationship with the Father, who has lived close to Him, who knows what it is to know God's grace and mercy, but for whatever reason decides, "I don't want to be here anymore. I want to run away. I want to escape." That kind of thinking inevitably leads to terrible and self-destructive choices.

The book of Proverbs in the Old Testament describes the contrast between two polar opposites: wisdom and foolishness (folly). Those are two contrary philosophies that inform two distinct lifestyles.

You can live a wise life. *"The fear of the Lord is the beginning of wisdom."*[15]

Or you can have a foolish life. *"A person's own folly leads to their ruin, yet their heart rages against the Lord."*[16]

How many times do we make choices and blame things on God and the circumstances God allowed when if we're honest, it was really our own choice? That's the story of the younger son in the story Jesus told.

"Not long after that, the younger son got together all he had, set off for a distant country and there he squandered his wealth in wild living."[17]

Sometimes the only way a person can learn is the hard way. We have to know that. Sometimes we can learn by watching and by precept, but many of life's toughest lessons have to be learned through difficulty. This story reminds us of God's willingness to allow us to make bad choices. This is the essence of the story. Everything flows to this and flows from this. In this one verse, it tells us he left, he took his stuff, he went a long way away (the far country, according to one translation), and there he squandered (wasted) his wealth in wild living. This is a picture of the road to ruin.

There are several markers on this road—signs that we should understand. We have a war raging within us. I heard it described like this when I was a kid: It's like you have two dogs inside you. You have one dog that's always barking about doing the wrong thing and another dog that wants you to do the right thing. It's the dog you feed that's going to be the strongest. That's profound because if you feed the spiritual nature, you'll be stronger spiritually. On the other hand, if you continue to feed the fleshly nature, that flesh will, at least momentarily, be stronger.

Desperation

This is the first marker on the road to ruin. This was a desperate young man. I'm going to parse this verse now from the classic King James. It talks about *"Soon thereafter,"* and, *"Not many days after."* In other words, this is a young man in a hurry. Sometimes that's a good thing. I have a biography of Winston Churchill titled *Young Man in a Hurry.* Paul, Saul of Tarsus, was also a young man in a hurry. He had ambition. He wanted to go places. We all know people who are ambitious, people who seem to be going places. Even earlier than most people figure life out, they've figured it out. They're steps ahead of other people. There are times in our lives to be decisive and to be quick, but more often than not when we are in a fever pitch of desperation, it's not a good thing.

The word *lust* in the Bible, which we usually associate with sexual immorality, is actually a common term in the Greek language. It's a synonym of the word *covet,* and it means desire or *over-*desire. It's a longing—a burning desire. You can have a lust for money. You can have a lust for power. There are a lot of things we can lust after inappropriately, and they always include a measure of haste. "I have to have this, and I have to have it now." Instant gratification. We want it now.

Karen and I are grandparents. We have seven grandchildren, ages seven years to eighteen. We had three daughters and no sons. We have six grandsons, one granddaughter. Five grandsons live nearby and are at our house pretty much all the time, so we are very involved with our grandchildren. These children like our house because it's "Day's house," "Day" being Karen's grandma name. Our oldest grandson is named David, and when he would hear Karen calling me across the house when he was a year old, "Dave, Dave, Dave," he associated that D-A phonetic sound with her, started pointing at her and calling her "Day." She thought, "That's a cool grandma name," so she ran with it. That's why she's called Day.

When the grandkids are over, they call out, "Day," constantly. It's like summoning a genie from a bottle. She's supposed to appear in front of them instantly, and if she doesn't appear, their voices escalate. "Day... Day... Day!" It's the most absurd thing. They never call Grandpa, I'm not there. Day is the sun; I am one of Neptune's moons. I am one of those far, distant planets out there. You know the one. I'm hardly noticed. They love to call Day because Day equals instant gratification. She's "Day on demand." These kids are going to grow up thinking they should have everything at their fingertips, on demand, because of Day. "I want a Pop Tart!" "Well, you just ate dinner five minutes ago!" "But I'm hungry. I want a Pop Tart." Instantly, Pop Tarts appear. That's the world they live in.

Actually, it's the world we *all* live in.

Think about modern living compared to long ago—for example, in the days of Noah. After his life peaked with that whole flood thing and surviving, he became bored and thought about what life was like before the flood. Maybe he remembered wine. "Remember that good wine we drank that time? We don't have any wine anymore. Boy, I could go for some wine." So what did he do?

"Noah, a man of the soil, proceeded to plant a vineyard."[18]

There's nothing "instant" about that. It was a process—a slow process. But now, everything is at our fingertips. Instant gratification versus deferred. This prodigal son was all about now. In the moment. How I feel now. What I want now. I must have it now.

Depreciation

This is the next marker on the road to ruin. I want you to think about this. The younger son gathered all of his stuff together. Now remember, the father gave his estate to both of his sons. In other words, he took himself out of the picture. So not only did the younger son get his inheritance, the older son got his as well—which was twice as much (two-thirds, one-third, according to the laws of inheritance at that time).

The father signed it all over to them. The estate was likely comprised of land and animals. The younger son inherited some of the flock, the herd, some of the real estate, but it doesn't say he carried all those things into the far country. He wanted to travel light. So what did he have to do? He had to convert as much as he could of what he received from the father to something liquid and lightweight. Cash. He must have had a fire sale. Maybe the elder brother got some good deals. Maybe he was able to purchase stuff from his kid brother for pennies on the dollar. Maybe other people around him got some good deals. All we know is this: The father had worked hard all his life. He gives the appropriate legacy to his younger son, and the younger son immediately liquidates it, devalues it, and is left with a much smaller share than to begin with, than what he would have had.

The road to ruin, the folly of disobeying God, is always going to leave you with less than you thought. The inflation rate, the attrition rate, the depreciation rate is not just incremental—it is *exponential.*

Desertion

The younger son started his journey. He headed toward a "distant country"—someplace far away. He didn't want to go to the next town over, the next property over, or the next county over; he wanted to get as far away as possible. That should give an indication of his folly. His journey was about farther and further—the former being about distance, the latter about degree.

I've often said if I could be transported in time to another era because I'm a student of preaching and preachers, I would want to go back about 150 years ago or so to the heyday of preaching in England during the Victorian Era. Men such as Charles Haddon Spurgeon, F.B. Meyer, Joseph Parker, and General William Booth of The Salvation Army, preached from pulpits, platforms, and even on the streets of London.

Then 200 miles north in Manchester, you could listen to one of the best preachers of any age. His name might not ring a bell, but if you know anything about the history of preaching, this man was a pulpit giant: Alexander Maclaren. For 45 years, he pastored in Manchester. At the time he pastored there, Manchester was considered the single most powerful and influential industrial center in the world. He was a tremendous expositor. One of the best pieces of advice I ever heard early on in my preaching career had to do with Maclaren. I was advised never to read his sermon on a particular text until my message from that text had already been prepared, because you'd be tempted to ditch your own outline and use Maclaren's. I have more than thirty volumes of his sermons in my library.

Preaching was Maclaren's primary work. Many today would not want him as their pastor because he focused solely on the ministry of the Word and little else. He didn't visit the flock. He didn't do "events" or "meetings." He didn't really interact with the people a lot. He felt like his main job was to work all week long so he could preach the Word on Sunday. He had his office at home, and the story is told that when he would enter that office early in the morning, he'd be dressed in his robe and his night clothes and his slippers. He would take his slippers off and work boots on to remind himself he was going to *work*—the hard work of study and preparation. He didn't do "Saturday night specials" pulled off the Internet. He worked hard on the text, and the fruit was in evidence each Lord's Day.

This spiritual food has lasted all these decades since. I recently read part of one of his sermons about the prodigal son and came across this quote:

"Sin takes us far away from God, and the root of all sin is that desire of living to one's self which began the prodigal's evil course."[19]

The prodigal was certainly living for and to himself. In fact, it was all about self. So he gathered it all together. He was desperate. His assets were depreciated. He deserted his family by setting out for a distant place.

Rebellion

We all are rebellious people—it's our nature. We don't like to be told what to do, do we? Let's say you live near a school bus stop. Children gather, and you don't want them walking on your lawn or trampling your roses. Let me give you some advice—don't post a sign that says, "Do Not Walk On My Grass," because it will have the opposite impact. Kids who had never even noticed your house before, much less the lawn, will find an excursion onto your property almost irresistible. This is because of an elementary part of human nature. We have a bias toward rebellion—it's our default position. In fact, the Bible is clear that the law of God was given not just to show us a standard for living, but also to prove a point—that we are sinners who need God's mercy and grace.

The far country is also a place of…

Relocation

Sometimes people think, "I just need a change of scenery. If I just get a new job, if I just get a new place to live, if I just get a new spouse… I'm going to relocate and change everything." Now, sometimes it's a good idea to relocate. God calls us to other places. I was called here to Fairfax. I relocated because God wanted me to do it. I prayed about it. It wasn't done in haste. I wanted to make sure it was the will of God.

In 12-step programs, they talk about people who look for a *geographical* cure. In other words, they have a problem that's in their own heart and life, but they feel like, "If I just go to this place and move to this place and start over…" but they notice they take the problem with them where they go.

Do you have a problem? Changing your address, changing your job, changing the scenery, changing your relationship is not going to fix a problem that's deep in your heart. That's the far country. It's a place of…

Reinvention

"I can go there, nobody knows me, and I can totally reinvent myself. I can start over." There's an allure to that. Years ago, early in my ministry, there was a pastor in a particular area who was notorious. He had pastored several churches, and he was a nothing short of a con-artist and predator. He had a series of adulterous affairs, and he got thrown out of church after church, and then lost his ministry, lost his family, lost his marriage. Years later, I was in another place and all of a sudden, I recognized a picture and it was the same guy. He was pastoring a church, but he had a *new* name. Why did he do that? So he could reinvent himself, and his past wouldn't follow him.

I think reinvention can be a good thing if it means *growth*. I've had to reinvent myself a lot. In ministry, God has challenged me. I've had to learn new styles of things. I've had to push myself and reinvent certain things. That's not a bad thing. We don't want to be stuck in a rut. I get that. When I was first a pastor, you would not have caught me without a suit and a tie and wingtip shoes. Seriously. I mean, I slept in those things because that's what a pastor looked like. That's what he wore. I had to come to a place where I realized what's important and what's not. Who am I trying to reach? Is it just about clothing? Is there Christian clothing? Somebody said to me, "Well, I think a preacher should dress up because the otherwise, you're just dressing like the world." I said, "Let me ask you a question. How does a banker dress?" "Suit and tie." "How does a lawyer dress? Aren't they the world?" So I had to think through things.

Debauchery

Debauchery is an old word for wicked living. We don't hear the term much these days, largely because culture has virtually dismissed moral norms as revealed in scripture. The death of Hugh Hefner in September 2017, and the way he was idolized in the media, highlighted this. He was a man consumed by lust and depravity. His "philosophy" glorified debauchery. My good friend, Cal Thomas, shared a powerful radio commentary about the pornographer:

"HUGH HEFNER, THE FOUNDER OF PLAYBOY MAGAZINE AND THE CAPTAIN OF THE SEXUAL REVOLUTION, IS DEAD AT 91. HIS LEGACY HAS RUINED LIVES AND FAMILIES, CAUSING MANY TO CONTRACT VENEREAL DISEASES, SOME OF WHICH HAVE NO KNOWN CURE. WHATEVER FANTASIES HE FULFILLED IN SOME MEN, HE LED THEM INTO A LIFESTYLE THAT WAS BAD FOR WOMEN AND CHILDREN AND EVENTUALLY THEMSELVES. THE TESTIMONIES OF WOMEN ASSOCIATED WITH HEFNER ABOUT HOW THEY FELT USED AND OFTEN DISCARDED LIKE SPOILED MEAT ARE SAD. IN THE MIDST OF A HEDONISTIC LIFESTYLE, HEFNER TOLD THE NEW YORK TIMES IN 1992: 'I'VE SPENT SO MUCH OF MY LIFE LOOKING FOR LOVE IN ALL THE WRONG PLACES.' HEFNER DIVORCED LOVE FROM SEX. HE TOLD MEN THEY COULD – AND SHOULD – HAVE SEX WITH ANY WOMEN THEY WISHED. NO WONDER WOMEN CAME TO COMPLAIN THAT MEN HAD TROUBLE COMMITTING TO THEM WHILE DATING OR MARRYING. HELEN GURLEY BROWN WAS THE FEMALE SIDE OF HEFNER, PREACHING THE SAME PHILOSOPHY TO WOMEN. IT ALWAYS ENDS IN DISAPPOINTMENT, IF NOT IMMEDIATELY, THEN IN ETERNITY. I'M CAL THOMAS IN WASHINGTON.[20]

There was a wonderful lady in my church in New York (now long with the Lord). Her name was Margaret Cook. Margaret made the best fried chicken and potato salad. She always made it for me on special occasions. One year, she was gone a couple of Sundays in February. She came back, and I told her that I had missed her. I asked, "Where've you been?" She said, "Well, me and some of my friends, we went down to New Orleans." They wanted to see what Mardi Gras was about. She said, "Pastor, I never saw so many naked (pronounced: 'neck ed') people in all my life!"

The Bible says the prodigal "wasted his substance with riotous living," Squandered it with wild living. It was a party. It was Mardi Gras every day.

"Do not get drunk on wine, which leads to debauchery. Instead, be filled with the Spirit."[21]

Peter talked about people living for God. He said:

"You spent enough time in the past before you were saved, doing what pagans choose to do living in debauchery, lust, drunkenness, orgies, carousing, and detestable idolatry. They are surprised that you do not join them in their reckless, wild living, and they heap abuse on you."[22]

Reckless, wild living. Debauchery. It started with desperation. Then some deals were made that depreciated his gifts. Then he set out to fulfill his fantasies, soon he was living a life of debauchery. He was on the road to ruin. My challenge to you, wherever you are in life, is this: are you home with the Father? Safe with him? Close to him? Stay there, but remember, I am prodigal. You are, too. We have the seeds of it. You can get hurt. You can get upset. You can get restless. You can become disillusioned. The next thing you know, you get desperate, and you start making choices that depreciate your gifts and abilities. Then maybe you desert, thinking, "I'm going to find a better place in life." It just swallows you up in a pit of debauchery. Everybody is somewhere on that curve.

CHAPTER THREE

Choices & Consequences

Everything bad happening in the world today, big or small, every injustice, every act of terror, every division, every expression of bigotry or racism, every time someone participates in something patently immoral, it all traces back to the concept of *sin*. God has set the standard. We're wired to function most efficiently in a certain way.

I have a car. A Chrysler Pacifica. Yes—a minivan. I thought I had outgrown such a vehicle, because my kids are adults. But I no longer have a real-man SUV. I lost the battle with my wife in hopes of one day owning a Range Rover, but we'll see what happens down the road. I don't know that that's ever going to happen.

In that boring minivan car, there is an owner's manual. That book is a guidebook. It tells me everything I need to know about the car. If I follow what the book says, because it was written by the people who built the car, things are going to be better with the car. If I just think I know better about the car (because I'm such a car person), I could get into trouble.

The Bible is the owner's manual for us. God owns us. He wrote it. He didn't sit up in heaven arbitrarily and say, "Oh, that looks like fun. I'll make it wrong." He didn't do that. He knows that built into every particular form of behavior, if it doesn't conform to why and how he created us, there are some built-in time-bombs—things that can hurt us. Sinful choices.

"After he had spent everything, there was a severe famine in that whole country, and he began to be in need. So he went and hired himself out to a citizen of that country, who sent him to his fields to feed pigs. He longed to fill his stomach with the pods that the pigs were eating, but no one gave him anything."[23]

Sinful choices are those we make that are contrary to what God has shown and told us. We can try to rationalize it away, but if God has spoken, it is clear.

Sinful choices lead to loss.

"After he had spent everything..."

This is the end of the road. The party is over. When he left home, he received a third of the estate, but he also had to liquidate some of it because a lot of it was real estate holdings and cattle. After all, he was not going to drive a herd of cattle to a distant land. He had to sell out for a reduced price.

He traveled with his wad of cash to the far country and lived as if there was no tomorrow. The proverb says, *"Where there is no vision, the people will perish."* That verse is often used as, "You have to have vision in ministry." What it really means is, "Where there is no direct revelation from God (in other words, when people don't take God seriously), the people cast off all restraint."[24]

The Russian novelist Dostoyevsky famously wrote, "If there is no God, everything is permissible."[25] So he's in the far country and he's spending. He's the life of the party. "Drinks on me!" We know he was living an immoral life, a life of debauchery. Now all the money is gone. He had spent everything. The first thing that happens, the first consequence to sin, is that sinful choices lead to *loss*.

You may think, "I'm on a winning streak," but when you're moving away from God, you're only going to win for so long. The Devil is only going to prop you up for so long; sin is only going to prop you up for so long. Eventually, you will lose. The universe will catch up with you. God will catch up with you. Commandments will catch up with you. The prodigal son lost everything: everything he had, everything his father had worked for.

It's sort of ironic. He went off to find his happiness thinking, "Oh, I'm going to be happy out there," not realizing because he was choosing to leave his father and disobey him to find his happiness, he was sacrificing something much more powerful and profound than happiness. His pursuit of happiness in the wrong places led to his loss of joy.

Joy and happiness are not the same—nor are they equal. Joy is something much deeper and much more pervasive, much more profound. When you start going away from that, you may find fleeting moments where you feel pretty happy, but you will never be able to tap into true joy. You will sacrifice joy on the altar of your misguided pursuit of what you perceive to be happiness.

That's why David, when he finally got right with God, after the sin with Bathsheba and all the complications, said, *"Restore to me the joy of your salvation and grant me a willing spirit to sustain me."*[26] Happiness is circumstantial. Happiness is fleeting. Joy can endure. Joy can be something pervasive. It's a well of water deep within. But when you turn your back on God, you short-circuit that capacity. You may find moments of pleasure, because there is pleasure in sin for a season. It's temporary. But sin and joy can never occupy the same heart.

You can also lose ultimate rewards. There is going to be a final judgment at the end of time for people who have rejected God. But believers are going to have our own unique judgment. It's when the Lord will reward us in heaven. It's called the judgment seat of Christ. What we're going to do is bring to Jesus our lives and what we've done with the gifts he gave us. Then he's going to sort through it and see what really mattered.

He says it this way in 1 Corinthians, chapter 3. *"If anyone builds on this foundation using gold, silver, costly stones, wood, hay, or straw..."* Let me stop there. What he's saying is, basically, you build your life using materials. Some of it is gold, some of it is silver, some of it is precious stones, some of it is wood, hay, or straw. In other words, there's some stuff we do that really matters (that's the gold, and the silver, and the precious stones). The wood, hay, and straw is the stuff that doesn't matter. At the end of our lives, that's the stuff you're going to wish you hadn't wasted time on. *"...their work will be shown for what it is* [at that judgment], *because the Day* [judgment day] *will bring it to light. It will be revealed with fire, and the fire will test the quality of each person's work."*[27]

So just imagine there's a big platform and there is some gold, there is some silver, there are some diamonds, and then there are some sticks and hay and kindling, and it's all ignited. Within a matter of moments, the wood, the hay, and the stubble is going to be burned up and gone. The other stuff is going to withstand the fire and maybe even be made purer.

He's saying, "Invest in the things that really matter, the gold standard." In other words, doing the will of God. *"If what has been built survives, the builder will receive a reward."* God will say, "Look at how much gold, silver, and precious stone. I'm going to give you a reward."

I'm enjoying watching my youngest grandson, Sawyer, in Little League because it's the first time he's at the stage where they keep score; they can actually win the game. I'll never forget when my grandson, Vinny, was at tee-ball or something and they said, "Just remember here, kids, everybody's a winner!" He just said, "Well, that means everybody is a loser too!" Vinny had it all figured out.

I understand we have to teach sportsmanship, but I always kept score at tee-ball, too. I just did. I wrote them down. I have it (for the permanent record). At the end of Sawyer's games, if two or three players have done outstanding work, they actually separate them out and give them an award for that. Now I know that's not very communistic. I know that's not very egalitarian. Everybody gets something. Nobody gets shunned. But if somebody does a really good job, he might get more. Rewards are okay. In fact, they are good. And they are not always equal—even with God.

Let me ask you a question. You're at work and Christmas bonus time comes (if there are bonuses). Do you want one? If another guy you perceive doesn't work as hard as you do gets a bigger one, does that bother you? "Oh, no. I'm a Christian. It wouldn't bother me." Sure. Sure. But Christians are going to get rewards. Listen. He says, *"If it is burned up, the builder will suffer loss but yet will* [still] *be saved, even though only as one escaping through the flames."* Some people are going to be barely saved.

You say, "Well, I'm there." Yeah. But when you get there and you realize Jesus died for you to get you there, wouldn't it be better for him to say, "Boy, I'll tell you what. You did good. You did good. You're not perfect, but you did good. I gave you some gifts and abilities and gave you some opportunities and you seized them and used them for my glory."

You say, "What's the fire?" The Apostle John on the Isle of Patmos in the book of Revelation, saw Jesus glorified and he said, "His eyes were as a flame of fire."[28] I believe the fire is the penetrating gaze of Jesus. Did you ever have somebody in your life like your grandma or your mom who could just look at you and melt you? Can you imagine Jesus? Can you imagine the look of disappointment in Jesus' eyes because you didn't use what he gave you?

Sinful choices lead to trouble.

"There was a severe famine in that whole country, and he began to be in need." He doesn't have anything; he's lost it all. There was a famine, and he began to be in need. The word *need* there is translated want. It's the Greek word *hysteria*. This is what it means: He began to freak out. He was messed up. "What am I going to do?"

Everybody has trouble. But if you don't manage and control the things God tells you to control in your life and manage for his glory, when things come along that are out of your control (big things; they happen in the world), those big out-of-control things will hit you harder because you haven't controlled what he gave you.

In other words, in a time of famine, in a time of downturn, if you have had a pattern of obeying God, you will get through it better than the ungodly person—every time. Everybody suffers in a famine. But the best preparation for that is to do what God would have you to do because you're going to have a more stable, balanced life. If you've messed up, you've squandered your life away and haven't lived for God and then the inevitable big downturn comes, the big kahuna of trouble, something you can't control, it'll nail you to the wall much more than it would have.

That's just a principle. You manage your life better. You're still going to experience a certain amount of pain. Famine is a very real thing. *Famine* basically means there's not enough food. There have been many, many famines. A couple hundred of them are recorded—major ones—in history. In our day and age, in the last few years, there have been famines in South Sudan. North Korea has experienced a terrible famine because of their regime. We know that.

I was recently reading a book about China during the Cold War, focusing on two particular periods: *The Cultural Revolution*, but before that, what was called the *Great Leap Forward*. That was when Chairman Mao Ze Dong wanted to really move China forward to become much more competitive among the industrialized nations of the world. He wanted to increase the output of grain and steel.

What it resulted in, basically, was a systemic failure of society. Historians tell us anywhere between 45 and 50 million people died in China between 1958 and 1962 under that system. Then came *The Cultural Revolution*. Many more people died in that bloodbath because communism is a system that cannot sustain itself.

Cycles come and go, I guarantee you. If you were living for God in 2006 and 2007, when 2008 hit, you were better equipped to handle it (even if you got hurt a bit) than somebody who had been living as if there was no tomorrow in 2006 and 2007. Trouble. The Bible says, *"Whoever sows injustice reaps calamity and the rod they wield in fury will be broken."*[29]

Let's look at another part of this verse. *"So he went* [after the famine] *and hired himself out to a citizen of that country, who sent him to his fields to feed pigs."* This is a terrible moment. Now remember, who is the audience? Pharisees? Publicans? Sinners? The Pharisees were obviously disgusted because the pig is an unclean animal. No Jewish person should have anything to do with this. He's going to feed pigs. That's how far he's gone.

Sinful choices lead to humiliation.

The younger son has totally humiliated himself. There's a difference between being humble and being humiliated. Humiliated is when we make choices contrary to God's plan and we embarrass ourselves. We've hit bottom. Sinful choices. You may think, "I'm riding high." You keep making those sinful choices and you're going to find yourself in a place where you are embarrassed and you feel humiliated. That's the shame.

Sinful choices lead to emptiness.

"He longed to fill his stomach with the pods that the pigs were eating..." Can you imagine how desperate this guy is? Now what does this mean? First of all, he longed. The word *longing* (King James says, *"...he would fain have filled his belly with the husks..."*) is the Greek word from which we get our English word lust, or covet. So he was *lusting* after pig food.

What were these pods? There was a particular tree indigenous to that part of the world (there's a cousin of it here in America today) and it produced carob pods. The pods were sort of like snow pea pods where there are several little seeds within this pod. The pod would hang on the tree. Inside this pod would be a few seeds. The seeds had some value because they were semi-sweet. This was like a poor-man's sweetener. It was a subsistence kind of thing. If you couldn't afford sugar or honey or something else, this is what you did. They would grind these seeds and make a primitive form of molasses out of them. The empty pods that were left over were not edible for human beings, but they were edible for pigs and they became a low-budget feed for pigs. In a famine, finding good quality feed for the animals would be hard. There was nothing sweet left in them. All the protein had been taken out. All that was left was the shell.

And those dried up and empty pods began to look pretty good to him.

Now there's another little situation here, and that is, if you're familiar with carob in American culture, sometimes carob is used in health food stores and other places as a substitute for chocolate. Karen's father really loved health food stores. GNC was his church (not really, he was a man of God). One day, he said, "Try this, Dave. You'll never want chocolate again." "What is it?" "They're carob seeds. Oh, they're good!" So I tried one. I thought I was going to die—honestly. "It's as good as chocolate, isn't it? It's better for you!" No, it wasn't. It's a poor substitute. Carob, as a substitute, is *a picture of the prodigal son who's settling for a poor substitute for something nutritious and real.* That's how far he had fallen. Sinful choices lead to emptiness. He's empty.

The sinful choices led to isolation.

The money was gone. The crowd was gone. You may not hit all of these on your way down, but I have to tell you. This is a pretty vivid picture. There are three things sin does to us. First, *sin makes us stupid*. Second, *sin makes us stubborn*. Third, *sin always eventually makes us sad*. It brings sorrow. It leads to isolation. You may wind up all by yourself

This is the moment that makes change possible. Eventually, the prodigal has a very decisive, *aha* moment, but there were things leading up to that. I believe there was a pattern of conviction leading to repentance. Think about this. This is a guy who has been sinning it up. He's been drinking, he's been in excess, he's been playing around with prostitutes, he's been living like the Devil, and it's all in him. He's been in a constant party, with a hangover every morning.

Now he had run out of money. He still may have wanted to do all of that stuff, but he had no money. There's no opportunity. He started to *detox*. If you've ever talked with people associated with *Alcoholics Anonymous* or other treatment programs, they say one of the first things the alcoholic has to do is stop drinking. Whenever I hear this, I say, "Duh!" What they mean is that stopping drinking is the only way to lift the fog from your brain so you can start thinking clearly about things you haven't been able to think clearly about.

I believe the fog was starting to lift from this prodigal son because he was not actively involved in those behaviors. He was not drinking. He was not even eating. There was nobody to hang out with. No money to pay for sin, because sin is expensive. So maybe he started hearing something.

Maybe he started hearing the father's voice.

A couple of years ago, Karen and I traveled up to Boston and were guests of an actor by the name of Blair Underwood who had recently acquired the rights to one of my novels. He was appearing in a play, and we wanted to get together and talk a little bit. It was a play called, *The Trip to Bountiful,* and he was appearing in it along with the actresses Cicely Tyson and Vanessa Williams. We went up there and we went backstage afterwards and met the cast. It was a cool experience.

But in that play, if you've ever seen the movie or play, *The Trip to Bountiful* (it was reprised at the Kennedy Center Awards a year or two ago), Cicely Tyson and someone else in the play sang a couple of old hymns. One of them was "Blessed Assurance," the old Fanny Crosby song.

The other hymn was a hymn written in 1880 by a man named Will Thompson.

Will Thompson was a very successful musician. He actually owned a company that put out music. Very successful. He was a nominal Christian, but one day he went to hear Dwight Lyman "D.L." Moody, the famous evangelist of the second half of the nineteenth century. The Lord got a hold of Thompson's heart, and he made a promise to God that he was going to use his talent for writing songs for Jesus after that.

Many of the hymns some of us grew up with, like, "Jesus is All the World to Me," and others were written by him. There was one that really became so special to the evangelist D.L. Moody. If you grew up ever watching any of the Billy Graham Crusades, Billy Graham always ended the crusade with an altar call and there was one song they sang more often than not. It was the great invitation song, "Just as I Am, Without One Plea."

Long before "Just as I Am," D. L. Moody chose as his "altar call" another song. In fact, when he was dying, he told Will Thompson, "I'd willingly trade everything I've ever done for Jesus if I could've just written that one song you've written." It was a song that whispered the mind of God. It was a song about how Jesus speaks to sinners, "Softly and Tenderly."

Softly and tenderly Jesus is calling,
Calling for you and for me.
See, on the portals, He's waiting and watching;
Watching for you and for me.
Come home, come home,
Ye who are weary come home;
Earnestly, tenderly, Jesus is calling;
Calling, "O sinner, come home!"
O for the wonderful love He has promised,
Promised for you and for me.
Though we have sinned He has mercy and pardon;
Pardon for you and for me.
Come home, come home,
Ye who are weary come home;
Earnestly, tenderly, Jesus is calling;
Calling, "O sinner, come home!"
Come home, come home,
Ye who are weary come home;
Earnestly, tenderly, Jesus is calling;
Calling, "O sinner, come home!"[50]

CHAPTER FOUR

Life-Change: A Case Study

Sam was an accomplished artist in the early part of the nineteenth century. If you look back at the iconic portraits of George Washington, often Sam was the artist. He was commissioned to do the White House portrait for President James Monroe. Sam made his living with commissions. People would pay him to paint important portraits. He was in Washington, D.C. in 1825, having been hired to do a portrait of the Marquis de Lafayette, who had helped so much during the American Revolution. It was while he was working on this painting that he received word about his wife, who had just given birth in New Haven, Connecticut. She was gravely ill. He immediately set out for home, but by the time he got there, she had passed. The message he had received had been carried by a messenger on horseback from Connecticut to D.C.

The news of her illness was more than a week old by the time poor Sam received it.

It was that moment that made Sam begin to think, "There has to be a better way to communicate." He had always been fascinated with electricity. People were just beginning to realize its potential. Soon thereafter, he had a conversation with someone who shared his interest, speculating about the possibility of transmitting electrical impulses along a wire. This idea blossomed, and eventually, he found someone in Congress to sponsor him.

In 1844, they ran a wire from Baltimore to Washington, D.C.—a wire to transmit short electric impulses. Sam developed a special code, turning the alphabet into various dots and dashes. The code was named after him — Samuel Morse. The first transmission made over that line from Baltimore to Washington, were the words, "What God hath wrought." Samuel Morse, in a sense, began the modern communication age with the idea, "There has to be a better way."

He had an *aha* moment.

There were other people who would have come up with some of these ideas, and other people who actually said they did. But it takes someone to be a pioneer in any game-changing industry. Imagine what our world was like before computers. Visionaries came along, and the same is true in every aspect of life. Those "*aha*" moments can be for good or for ill. They are life-changing moments.

In the context of the parable of the prodigal son, we have come to the inevitable point of the story, in a sense, where all the bad news, all the drift, all the decline, all the bad stuff begins to change. There's a turning point. There's a defining moment. There's a pivot that happens in the story.

One of my pet peeves is when people say, "Oh, people don't change. He'll never change. She'll never change." It's very dismissive. I would agree there are people who don't change. I would also concede changing is a pretty hard thing to do. But I will tell you, the whole reason we have a Bible and why everything in the Bible points to the finished work of Jesus Christ on the cross is because it establishes the fact that people *can* change.

We all change. We grow. That's change. *"We are all, with increasing glory from faith to faith, being changed into the image of our Lord,"* it says in 2 Corinthians, chapter 3. People can change. It's easy to get cynical— especially if you see someone ruining their life. "Oh, they'll never change." But that's not a sentiment made on the basis of faith or revealed truth. That's not a statement made on the basis of the promises of God. That's a statement based on doubt and cynicism, which are the polar opposite of Scripture.

"Jesus continued: 'There was a man who had two sons. The younger one said to his father, 'Father, give me my share of the estate.' So he divided his property between them. Not long after that, the younger son got together all he had, set off for a distant country and there squandered his wealth in wild living. After he had spent everything, there was a severe famine in that whole country, and he began to be in need. So he went and hired himself out to a citizen of that country, who sent him to his fields to feed pigs. He longed to fill his stomach with the pods that the pigs were eating, but no one gave him anything. When he came to his senses, he said, 'How many of my father's hired servants have food to spare, and here I am starving

to death! I will set out and go back to my father and say to him: Father, I have sinned against heaven and against you. I am no longer worthy to be called your son; make me like one of your hired servants.[31]

This is a picture of life-change—the moment when the wandering son turns his story around. There is no need for a spoiler alert; the story is not only familiar—it's predictable, especially if you know anything about the storyteller. It is that way with the great stories told throughout time. There's usually a crisis moment, a turning point, something that happens that changes the main character. There are several clear elements in this kind of transformation.

Life-change begins with CLARITY.

When he came to his senses, it was a moment of clarity. He saw things clearly. It was like Paul on the Damascus road. What a story of conversion. He was on the way to persecute and kill Christians. He saw the light. He heard the voice. We still refer to dramatic change as "Damascus Road" moments. It's a metaphor for dramatic life-change that happens suddenly.

We know from reading the context of the story that the prodigal's change didn't happen in a vacuum. It appears to have been instantaneous, but even in the most dramatically decisive moments of change, there's usually something else that's been happening for a while. In Saul of Tarsus's case, he had witnessed the sermon of Stephen before the Sanhedrin. He had also witnessed the martyrdom of Stephen.[32]

When Jesus talked to Saul in that moment of conversion, he mentioned how hard it was for him to kick against the goads.[33] In other words, he was being troubled or prodded in his conscience by how Stephen died and what he said about seeing Jesus standing at the right hand of God. It had convicting power. It was preparing him. So I believe it was with the prodigal son. There was a moment when he came to his senses, but something had been happening in his mind and heart long before his encounter as he approached the city of Damascus.

The prodigal son had hit bottom. The money was gone. The people were gone. The party was over. He was filled with desperation and hunger. Sin can be expensive, especially his particular sins of choice. Even if he wanted to continue doing them, he no longer had any money. For the first time since he left home, all the sinful toxins were being washed out of his system. He was doing some hard work. The first such work in a long time—maybe the hardest labor in his life.

And the fog began to lift.

As I mentioned earlier, many rehab or recovery programs last about a month. Part of the reason for this is that there is evidence it takes about twenty-eight days for someone to sufficiently detox from the physical effects of whatever substance they have been abusing. In other words, in order to get a person to a place where they can begin to think and reason clearly, because they've been under the control of this substance, they have to give it time to flush—or *detox*—their system.

It's the same with all sinful habits.

If you're involved in sin and you know it's sin, and it has control over you, the best thing you can do right now is to stop it. You say, "Well, wait a minute, Pastor. If I could stop it, I would." I'm not talking about stopping it in the sense of full repentance—that will and must come, eventually—but I mean stop the behavior long enough to clear your head and heart. Jesus said, "If your right hand offends you, cut it off. If your right eye offends you, pluck it out."[34] He was talking about adultery in that context, but the same is true about any moral shortcoming. He was talking about taking drastic action. More than 75 years ago, a term appeared in popular culture, when drug use began to become a national problem—particularly heroin. Trying to kick the habit immediately and drastically was called going "cold turkey."

I've counseled people throughout my ministry. I remember one time I was counseling a person who was having an adulterous affair. He said: "Okay, Pastor Stokes. I'm going to cut it off, so I'm going to go see her one more time for some closure." I said, "No, you're not. That's not how it works. It never works that way. You need to cut it off now and then find your 'closure' later. The other party in the immoral relationship will never be part of that process. It's going to hurt, but that's part of the cure." You have to stop because until you get the sinful feelings out of your system—at least to an extent—you're never going to be able to process all the good stuff that must become part of your new, repentant life.

Aha moments are the stuff of movies and literature. One of my favorites was from the classic movie *The Bridge on the River Kwai*, when the British officer, played by the brilliant actor Sir Alec Guinness, realized how he had helped the enemy by putting so much effort into leading the prisoners in the effort to build a crucial bridge. At the key moment, the light came on and he utters the words, "What have I done?" He then staggered toward the plunger and blew up the bridge.

Jesus said, "*When* he came to his senses." I'm struck by that word. In one translation it says, "And," not the conjunction *but*. It's almost like a continuation of the story. I find some comfort in it. Maybe I'm reading too much into it. Remember, there are two applications to this parable. It's all about people far from God. One is somebody who has never had a relationship with God. They're far. They need to have a first relationship. That's one application. That's getting saved.

The other is you used to have a close relationship, but you're moving away from God and you come back. It's this second one I want to speak to: If you're truly saved and you have the Holy Spirit living within you and you wander off and you rebel, it is not a matter of *if* you're going to come back to God, it is a matter of *when* you're going to come back to God. The big question is how long will you wait? How much damage will you do because of your delay? Because you're going to come back. God is never going to let you go.

Recently, at a shopping mall near my home, I watched a mother with her hand on her little girl like I used to walk with my daughters when they were young. The little girl wanted to go to a particular store, but not the mother. You know how kids are. She started dragging her feet. This kid was just dragging along. I thought, "This child is going to lose the battle because her mommy is stronger."

It's like that in our walk with God.

God has you by the hand. You may drag your heels and scream and yell and look the other way, stick your tongue out at him, but when God wants you to go somewhere, he's going to get you there. I've had people describe wandering from God like, "I don't know why I was doing stuff, Pastor. It's like I had an out-of-body experience and I was watching myself be stupid."

As I've said, sin makes you *stupid*, sin makes you *stubborn*, and sin always makes you *sad*. Let me add this one, sin also always works on your *sanity*. Sin makes you crazy. You're doing crazy stuff. People are saying, "That person is crazy." No. They're just in sin. They're not thinking clearly.

"He came to himself" is how the King James Version reads. This would be the opposite of to be beside yourself. When the demon-possessed maniac was healed in Mark chapter five, all the people saw him sitting clothed and in his *right mind. "God has not given us a spirit of fear,"* Paul told Timothy, *"but of love and power and of a sound mind."*[85] *"Gird up the loins of your mind."*[86] Gird, like girdle. Wrap up the loins of your mind. Get control of your thinking.

When you start to think clearly, you are on your way to life-change.

Life-change involves CALCULATION

He made this calculation: *"How many of my father's servants have food to spare, and I'm starving to death?"* He actually did the math. Have you done the math on the consequences of sin? It's only when you're thinking clearly that you can actually see how that all works out because all you've been thinking about is pleasure and self. But now, there's a new calculation. There's a new reckoning. It's a calculation that says, "Look at where I am and look at how even the lowest person on Dad's payroll lives." That's the calculation. But you have to have a clear mind to make it. Only when you have that clear mind can you begin to see sin and its consequences rather than its attractive, seductive elements.

Life-change involves CONVICTION

"I will set out and go back to my father." This is the crucial moment because there are many times a person has clarity and even calculation, but they don't let it develop into *conviction*. Let's consider two case studies: Judas and Peter.

Judas betrayed Jesus. Peter denied Jesus. We could argue all day, "Which one was worse?" but I think there is a moral equivalency. I think to deny Jesus three times while he was going through what he was going through was a form of betrayal. Judas and Peter both experienced guilt. Both men eventually regretted what they did. They had *aha* moments.

Judas threw the money back and went out and killed himself.

Peter wept bitterly, repented, and on the day of Pentecost several weeks later preached a sermon and 3,000 people were converted.

What was the difference? One took his guilt and carried it to the *grave*. One took his guilt and carried it to *grace*. That's all. That's the conviction. At some point in life-change, no matter how bad you feel about something, you have to say, "I will arise. This is what I'm going to do. I have to do something about this." It's hard because you don't feel like that at first. Remember what I was talking about, the eye and the hand being cut off? You don't feel like that.

If you go back 75 or 80 years and look at interviews where people were asked their opinion, invariably, in print, you'll see somebody ask, "What do you think about President Roosevelt's handling of the economy?" The reply would likely start, "Well, here's what I *think*." If you ask the average person today for an opinion on something, nine times out of ten the reply will involve, "Here's what I *feel*." We're a whole nation and world of uncontrolled feelings. Feelings drive everything. "You hurt my feelings." "Well, that's how I feel," end of discussion. I love something that Martin Luther wrote 500 years ago:

> *For feelings come and feelings go,*
> *And feelings are deceiving;*
> *My warrant is the Word of God —*
> *Naught else is worth believing.*

I'll trust in God's unchanging Word
Till soul and body sever,
For, though all things shall pass away,
His Word shall stand forever!

Years ago, there was a popular Gospel pamphlet titled, "Safety, Certainty, and Enjoyment." It was about the assurance of salvation. It had a train with an engine, one car, and a caboose. On the engine was the word fact, F-A-C-T. On the second car was the word faith. On the third car was the word feeling. What the pamphlet taught is what has to drive everything is truth. What are the facts? What are the promises? What did God say? We have faith in God's facts. Then feelings come along—sometimes much later.

I wake up some mornings and I don't feel saved. In fact, I don't usually feel all that spiritual until I've had a couple of cups of coffee. People say, "I got up this morning and said, 'This is the day the Lord hath made!'" Not me. It takes a while sometimes. If you doubt your salvation, are you basing that on how you feel or on the facts? Look at God's facts, what he has said, even if you don't feel that way. Have faith in the fact and you know what will happen? The feeling will come along.

Our feelings are always lagging indicators. We can change our feelings. I spoke to someone recently and conducted an experiment to illustrate this truth. We were talking about food that makes us ill. She said, "Oh, salmon makes me sick." So I began to dialogue with her. "After church, somebody needs to take you over to this great restaurant. They have a wonderful salmon dish. Order it medium rare so it's really oily." After just a few moments her stomach started to turn. Her feelings changed—because of what she was thinking.

Think about the last time somebody cut you off in traffic. Think about it right now. Just pause and think. All of a sudden you had a feeling, didn't you? It wasn't a Christian feeling. You see, thoughts produce feelings. We think we're just slaves to feelings. "Oh, that's just how I feel. I can't control it." Sure, you can!

Change your thinking, and you will change your feelings.

If you're thinking about something negative, think about something positive. If you're thinking about something ugly, think about something beautiful. If you're thinking about that neighbor who's in the HOA and they've written you up for your trash being out front too early one time (again), think about one of your grandkids. Change the feeling.

Don't settle for the lie that feelings are ultimate and perpetual. They're not. If you base your life on feeling, you're never going to be consistent about anything.

Life-change requires CONFESSION

If you're going to have the conviction that leads you to arise and go back to the Father, you're going to have to verbalize some thoughts. What does he say? *"I have sinned against heaven and against you."* Sin. Never hesitate to call it *sin*. Sinful choices. He demanded an inheritance. That was sin. He was a poor steward of what he had been given. That was sin. He repudiated the father. That was sin. He wandered into the far country. That was sin. While he was there, he just poured it on. Sin, sin, sin, sin.

You're never going to experience life-change until you're willing to confess your sins. What did he say? "I'm going to tell Dad this." He was planning it out. There are a lot of lessons in this. If you really want to do something right, plan out exactly what you want to say. People tell me, "I want to go make something right with a person." Then write down exactly what you want to say. Plan it out. Leave nothing to chance.

"I will arise and go to my father and say, 'I have sinned. I have sinned against heaven and against you.'" Do you see that order? You're never really going to change your life if all you see are the horizontal consequences of your choices. They may be very real. They may be vivid. They may haunt you. But real life-change begins when you see its vertical impact. Sin, first and foremost, is an affront to the God who loves you.

Did you ever notice the difference between the stories of David and Bathsheba and Joseph and Potiphar's wife? Joseph was probably about 19 or 20 years of age, a young man; arguably a stronger sex drive than David in his fifties. But David sinned with Bathsheba, and Joseph ran from Potiphar's wife. Do you remember why Joseph ran? He didn't say, "Well, it's a sin against Potiphar's wife. It's a sin against Potiphar." That's not what he said. He said to her, "How can I commit such a sin against God?"[37]

David didn't think about how his behavior would impact God until a year or so after he messed up so badly. Only then did he see his sin vertically. He prayed, *"Against you, you only, have I sinned, O Lord.'*[88] He had sinned against Bathsheba. He had sinned against Uriah. He had sinned against his nation. He had sinned against the baby who was born. But he said, "Against you, you only."

You see, you have to have a view of what sin does to God. You say, "Well, how do I know?" Watch *The Passion of the Christ*. It's imperfect, but watch the beating and the brutality of the crucifixion and realize Jesus had to go through that because of our sins. "I've sinned against heaven and against you." If he'd had gone back and said, "Dad, I messed up. I sinned against you," I know the father would have probably said, "And more importantly, you sinned against God."

Unless you get right with God first, until you get the vertical, you'll never have the horizontal completely in place. You'll never be able to love your neighbor as yourself until you do the first commandment, to love God with all your heart and all your soul and all your mind.

CHAPTER FIVE

From SHAME to GRACE

This is the point in the story when the wayward son begins the journey to his new life. He hits the road and moves from shame and toward grace. The imagery is amazing. He has been far from home and the father. It's a compelling picture of someone being far from God. This can mean you're far from God because you've never been close to God in the first place. Or it can apply to someone who has previously been close to the father, but has strayed—wandered off. But this parable is not just about the sons—it's also very much about the father.

That's what Jesus was trying to teach his audience at the time, which was comprised of three groups: The publicans, who were the very up-and-out sinners, the outcasts of society; the sinners, who were the down-and-out, and then the Pharisees, who were religious but lost. You can be very, very religious but not know God. In fact, religion, many times, is a barrier to authentic faith. So if you're far from God in that sense, it's a story about God's desire to have this relationship with you.

Then it can apply (as it does, and many people identify with the story in this way) that you used to be close to God but you're not as close to God as you once were. You've drifted. You've wandered. Maybe you've rebelled. The world, the flesh, the Devil has distracted you and it's about finding your way back to that place of home and closeness and fellowship with God. Clean, clear, close. I often talk about those as values. Being clean before God, being clear about God's plan for your life, and being close to God.

Now that the prodigal son had hit bottom and his thinking started to clear, he made a decision. He no longer had any money to party with so he was not hungover all the time. His mind was starting to clear up. He said:

"I will set out and go back to my father and say to him: Father, I have sinned against heaven and against you. I am no longer worthy to be called your son; make me like one of your hired servants."[89]

This is interesting because he was not only demonstrating vital humility, he was also describing the concept of *restitution*. We can assume that such a young Jewish boy had been taught by the rabbis about restitution. If you do something wrong, you make it up to that person. His journey back home was not, in his mind, just about reconciliation—it was also about restitution. He was determined to make the wrong thing right. There was a debt. He wanted to go back and work it off. He thought, "I have to be willing to do this. I don't have any money to pay my father back, but I will work it off." It was the crucial part of his decision.

It's not enough to wake up. It's not enough to have a moment where you start to see clearly. It's not even enough to know what you need to do. You know exactly the road you need to take. You have to do what it says in the first sentence of the next verse. *"So he got up and went to his father."*[2]

All of the great spiritual breakthroughs in life—faith, repentance, and even reconciliation—require an action step. There was something he had to do. *Faith* is conviction based on revelation that leads to action. That last part is important. Every time in the Bible someone is commended for their faith (Hebrews 11, the great roll call of faith), they had faith and *they did something*. Abel offered a more excellent sacrifice by faith. Noah built an ark by faith. Moses led the people through the parting of the Red Sea. People acted on conviction. They were totally convinced because of God's promises. *Revelation* means God has revealed, God has commanded, God has promised, and God has accomplished.

It's not enough to be emotionally "moved"—we must put emotion into obedient *motion*.

You have to be willing to take action. The old illustration is so simple. There's a chair. I ask you if you believe the chair can support you. You reply, "Sure." But are you willing to sit down on the chair to prove it? That's faith—conviction in motion. It's not enough to believe God can hold you up. Are you willing to be seated with him in faith? All life change involves an action step. What's the one you need? If you want to make something right with another person, you need to take action and move toward that person. Sometimes the action is a painful action. Sometimes someone is involved in an addiction. They have to change a habit. They have to go cold turkey. Just tough it out.

Jesus was talking about this when he said, "If your right hand offends you, cut if off. If your right eye offends you, pluck it out."[40] That's pretty much cold turkey. He's not advocating mutilation. What he's saying is to take severe action.

If there's a relationship that's dragging you down and you know it's improper, cut it off. Don't feed it. You might say, "Well, it'll feel bad for a while." Sure, it will. Have you ever talked to someone who has lost a limb describe "phantom" pain? The limb that is gone, but they still feel nerve pain where it once was.

You will still feel pain even after you cut something off, but you're never going to cure the problem with that cancerous, diseased appendage in your life—something sinful. You have to stop it.

One of the greatest comic videos I've ever seen involves Bob Newhart, who played a psychologist on *The Bob Newhart Show*. He's a funny guy. Somebody went to Bob Newhart for counseling. She mentioned several problems. Newhart listened to this lady describe one of them in great detail. Then he says, "Well, I have a cure for you." She said, "Oh, great! Can I write it down?" He says, "Well, you could, but you don't have to. It's two words." She says, "Okay. What's the cure?" He says, "*Stop it!*"

I have to tell you, I have counseled for years, and that's what you want to say sometimes—just stop it! Is it easy?

No, of course not. It's painful. But you're never going to get back to the father's house until you get up and go in that direction. You have to take action. You have to get up and go.

In the classic King James Version, the text says, *"He arose and went to his father."* You can't miss the imagery. It's like a resurrection moment. I think you're most tapped in to what Paul described in Philippians 3:10 as the power of the resurrection of Jesus when, in obedience to the will of God, you turn your life around. Repentance means change. Change of mind, change of heart that leads to a change of direction that leads to a change of destiny. When you change and you turn, it is a form of resurrection.

There's terminology in baseball. I grew up in the Detroit are listening to the late Ernie Harwell, a Hall of Fame broadcaster, who for decades was the voice of the Detroit Tigers. His words created images in my mind as I followed the games on my transistor radio. There would be a runner on first. Harwell would say something like, "Whitey Ford is looking over at first base, and he throws over there and Kaline moves back to first base." Kaline, not really a great speedster, was trying to figure out whether to break and try to steal.

At some point, Kaline thought he was reading the left-hander correctly and thought he could steal second. He made a move and the pitcher threw behind him, picking him off. Here's how Harwell described it: "Ah, he caught Kaline leaning!" I love that phrase—"caught him leaning." I love it because some of the great breakthroughs in our lives happen when God catches us leaning, because when God catches us leaning, He takes us the rest of the way. You take the first step. He will take care of all of the rest.

The prodigal was on his way home. Maybe along the way he saw things that reminded him of what a knucklehead he had been. It's a painful journey, but he was starting to draw close. *"But while he was still a long way off, his father saw him and was filled with compassion for him; he ran to his son, threw his arms around him and kissed him."*[41] Wow. What a picture of love. He's still a long way off. His father sees him, has compassion, runs to him.

Why does his father see him? Because the father has been looking for him to come back ever since he left. Jesus came to seek and to save that which was lost. God sees because He's looking. He's always watching. This is not a serendipitous moment. The father's attention was deliberate.

I'm not much of one for New Age stuff, certainly not a fan of pop psychology, but I do believe there is a place in life (I've seen this work many times, and I've counseled people this way) where somebody you love has rebelled against God, and all you can do is pray for that person. Everything you've tried to do doesn't work. It's now in the hands of God. It's like that famous Serenity Prayer: *"God, grant me the serenity to accept the things I cannot change, the courage to change the things I can, and the wisdom to know the difference."*

One of the best things you can do is get an image in your mind of what that person would look like being right with God and fully back to where he or she ought to be. When you pray for that person, keep that image in your mind, because that's an image that's based on hope. When you pray for someone who is hurting, praying in faith for their healing, see them as healed. You say, "Well, will God heal them or not?" That is up to God. I'm not talking about a psychological thing that's going to change that. But I'm saying, if you have faith, see them as restored.

Many years ago, when I was pastoring in the St. Louis area, I was going over some names—recent visitors to our services—and I saw a card from somebody who had visited our service three or four weeks earlier and hadn't been back since. His name was Roland. I saw the address, noticed it was in a trailer park. Right then the Lord began to impress on me to visit him immediately. I thought, "This is crazy. First of all, he's not home. He's working. And I have stuff to do." But the impression from the Lord stayed with me. Finally, I couldn't resist it. So I began to pray, "Is this something you want me to do?" The Lord put an image of this man in my mind.

All I remember about this man was he was a big fellow and he had a mustache. I'd shaken his hand one time in the service and said, "Hello," maybe. But I knew enough to put a face with the name—barely. Then I had an image in my mind where both of us were kneeling down in his trailer in an act of prayer. So I'm getting a little Twilight Zone-ish because I was a life-long Baptist. We don't do that. We believe healing happens, but only with Paul, not us. That kind of thing. God doesn't work that way with Baptists. We know that.

I got in my car and drove over to the trailer park. I found the right trailer and knocked on the door (part of me was hoping he wasn't home). Roland answered the door. I said, "Hi, Roland, I'm…" He interrupted, "I know who you are, I've been to your church." I said, "Yes, you were." I said, "This is going to be the weirdest thing, but I just felt impressed to come by and talk to you this morning. May I come in?"

I went in and talked a little bit, made some small talk about the Cardinals and baseball and a bunch of different stuff. They had just won the World Series in '82. I finally said, "The reason I'm here, actually, is to talk to you about some spiritual things." I asked him, "Do you know for sure you have a relationship with God? Let me ask you a question." This is what we used to say all the time. "Do you know that if you died today you'd go to heaven?"

They taught us that in evangelism in the 70s, to ask people if they're going to die today—scare them to death. That's the best way to get them saved. Just scare them to death. Right? "You might die in the next two minutes. If you do, are you saved?" Hold a gun on them, "You might die. Are you saved?" "Yes, Lord! I'm saved!" He said, "No, but I've been thinking about it some." I pulled out a New Testament and shared with him some scriptures from the book of Romans.

Then I said, "You could invite the Lord Jesus into your heart right now. What would you think about praying with me right now?" I remember I didn't say "kneeling and praying with me." He said, "I'd love that." He got up from his seat and he knelt in front of his chair. I knelt next to him. He was gloriously saved. And it was the very image that had been in my mind—the one I believe the Lord planted there earlier that morning.

What's my point? The father was watching, and he saw his son in the distance. This didn't surprise the father. Now, in this story, the father clearly represents God. He runs to meet his son. He embraces him. This was not what the son expected. He expected to have to jump through many hoops. Instead, he encountered *extravagant grace*.

In spite of the unexpected reception—the son didn't change his plan. He stayed on script. He said, "I've been practicing this. I know you're hugging me and all, but give me some space here." The son said to him, *"Father, I have sinned against heaven and against you. I am no longer worthy to be called your son."*[2] What do you think about that, Dad?" The father totally ignored it. Does that mean it was wrong to confess? No. It was right because remember, confession is not about us convincing God. It's about us *agreeing* with God and convincing ourselves, because God already knows our hearts.

"But the father said to his servants, 'Quick! Bring the best robe and put it on him. Put a ring on his finger and sandals on his feet.'" Now this was a guy who had left home with sandals, left with a ring, left with a robe, but by the time he came back, he's bedraggled, barefoot, having traversed mile upon mile. His feet were dirty and likely bleeding. He was probably dehydrated.

A robe, in Scripture, speaks of royalty. It also speaks of righteousness. In Revelation, it talks about robes of righteousness. He's basically saying, "Wrap this around him. Let him know he's making things right with me." "Bring the ring!" The ring is jewelry, but a ring meant something else in those days.

Do you remember when Joseph, the patriarch, interpreted the dream Pharaoh had, and it was the dream that there were going to be seven bad years after seven good years so they needed to save twenty percent of the grain to prepare for lean times? Pharaoh said, "I need somebody to run this thing." The bottom line is Joseph was the man. He gave him his signet ring, which was basically like giving somebody your ATM code, your number, your card. Giving him the authority. The ring had a seal on it. If there was a document, there would be some wax from a candle, and the seal would have the imprint of the ring, making it official. You see this throughout Scripture. It was the same of land owners and people who had holdings. In order to transact business, it became official when it was signed and the signet ring was used as a seal there.[43] So, when the father asked for a ring, he was not just asking for some jewelry—he was letting the son know, "I'm giving you my bank account number. I'm giving you my Visa card. You're restored to transact business in my name."

Then he said, *"Bring the fattened calf and kill it. Let's have a feast and celebrate."* Why? *"For this son of mine was dead and is alive again; he was lost and is found.' So they began to celebrate."*

Now there are some wonderful pictures here. Forgiveness. Let's think about forgiveness. I've told you often. I wrote about it in *When Good Samaritans Get Mugged.* When we forgive others, nine times out of ten (my statistic, but I think it's true), we are having to forgive someone who has not come to us asking for it. If you're only going to forgive people who are going to beg your forgiveness, you're never going to forgive much. You have to learn how to let things go with people who don't even ask you. Then, when someone does come and ask you, when someone takes that step to turn around and make something right with you, I think this story gives us a picture of how we should receive those people. We shouldn't say, "I don't know whether I can trust you." Maybe you can, maybe you can't. "Let's watch you for a while." No. When someone wants to be reconciled, you run and meet them and you embrace them. You trust that it is legit. The same is true with the church. A church ought to be a great place of celebration because it's filled with sinners—capable of all sorts of bad behavior.

I am prodigal.

Sometimes the sinners who make up the body of Christ slip back into old patterns. They wander off. They get hurt about something, or they get distracted by something, and they start making bad choices. They're gone, and it's sad. We should be praying for them to come back to God. We should have an image of that in our head. And then, when they come back and they walk in that front door and they've aged ten years in one, they smell like a brewery, their hair hasn't been combed, they've been rejected by loved ones. Lost jobs. Been through bad times. We must be affirming and embracing. The prodigal may not want anyone to see what sin has done to him, but we, like the father, look beyond that—he's home!

We ought to celebrate repentance. How many churches do you know that merely tolerate life change, and reserve their celebration for their own self-righteous selves? God help us.

CHAPTER SIX

Big Brother is Watching

Remember—this is a story about *two* sons. During his discourse with the Pharisees, publicans, and sinners, Jesus was using the common teaching tool of threes. A tip of the hat to Aristotle. He talked about a lost coin, a lost sheep, and finally, the lost son. That's three.

But look closer. He also uses the power of three in the finale, for there are really three prodigals in the parable. The first prodigal is the one who runs off. The word *prodigal* means extravagant, wasteful. It can be a positive or a negative. Then there's the prodigal father because he's *extravagant in his grace*. The third "prodigal" was the older son. He was extravagant in his opinion of himself. This part was aimed at the Pharisees.

"Meanwhile, the older son was in the field. When he came near the house, he heard music and dancing. So he called one of the servants and asked him what was going on. 'Your brother has come,' he replied, 'and your father has killed the fattened calf because he has him back safe and sound.'"[44]

Even in life's most positive moments, the dark cloud of negativism is nearby. Have you ever noticed that? Even when you're the happiest, something can happen to really deflate you. I find that in one word (it's a cool word): *meanwhile*. If ever you've seen an old movie or an old black and white television show—a western—something would be happening back out in a field someplace, and a caption or a narrator would say, "Meanwhile, back at the ranch..." It was a segue. It meant something was happening simultaneously. In our story, while the big party is going on, there was drama elsewhere.

"Meanwhile, outside..."

I'm not trying to beat you up with this, but I think it needs to be said. There are probably more people in this church at any given time who wrestle with the issues the older brother had more often than church people wrestle with the issues that impacted the younger. Sure, some may want to run from God, but many more wrestle with issues of criticism, pride, and holier-than-thou self-righteousness.

I heard it described some years ago, and it was really an eye-opening thing to me, because I had always thought that difficulty and trial and good times in life were cyclical. You'd have some good times, then you'd have an episode of bad times, then you'd have some good times. Some of it does happen that way, I guess. But I've also learned a lot of the time, good things are happening in our lives and bad things are happening around us in a parallel way. I think that's the far more difficult thing to handle.

H.B. London, Jr. started Pastor Appreciation Month when he was on the staff of Focus on the Family. I once heard him describe people he identified as the joy suckers in life. Have you had any joy suckers in your life? He's talking about in ministry, you get these people. You just see them coming. Their purpose in life is to suck all the joy out of you. If you're having a good day, you don't want to talk to them. Don't say, "How are you doing?" because they're going to tell you.

Here's a little rule of life. When someone says, "How're you doing?" they want you to say, "Really well." Even if you're just about dead, say, "Really well." Don't dump on them, because it's meant more as a courtesy. Don't be a joy-sucker. That's what the older brother was. I want you to know, when you have some of the greatest victories in your life, you'll start sharing that and testifying and you'll think you're going to get a good response. And someone you think ought to rejoice is going to say, "Oh, I don't know if I believe that."

A kid comes home from church camp and tells his dad, "Man, God spoke to me at youth camp, and I think I'm going to surrender my life to be a missionary," or, "I'm going to go off to Bible college and learn." A parent who has tithed, loved the Lord, taught Sunday School, loves Jesus, knows all the third verses of every old hymn says, "Well, I think you need to think this thing through. Are you sure?"

That sucking sound is joy going down the drain.

Here's another observation. True worship will always lead to service. *But serving itself doesn't always connect us to worship.* This is an important distinction. The older son was in the field. He was not at the party. He was not with the father embracing the son. You might want to say, "Well, somebody had to do the work. Somebody has to work around here." But that kind of criticism can turn toxic.

In this story, the father's house is a metaphor for fellowship and celebration and closeness to God. The field is a metaphor for being out in the field doing the work, like a missionary on a foreign field. Here's my observation, and I think it's true 100 percent of the time: If you begin as a worshipper, humbling yourself, daily surrendering yourself to God, and you worship God in spirit and in truth, you will always, not sometimes, not much of the time, but *always* find some kind of tangible work for the Lord Jesus Christ.

But there are many church people who would rather do something than to really get close to God Himself. They're much more comfortable out in the field doing hands-on work. "They're partying. They're celebrating. That's a waste of time. Look at that dancing and singing. Man, we have work to do out here in the field!" Of course, we need both—worship and work—but we must never use "good works" as a way to escape heart worship. I think there are even a lot of people in vocational ministry who actually are missionaries and pastors in the field doing the work, but they've long since disconnected from any real close relationship to God, and it becomes a slippery slope.

I had a recent conversation with my father—a retired pastor. That's right, I'm a "preacher's kid"—explains a lot, huh? Dad pastored churches in Michigan, the Detroit area. There was always a small group of men in the church—ushers, officers, etc.—and the custom in the church was that they would receive the offering and then they'd go to some secret place in the building to count it. They'd never, ever come into the church to worship and hear the sermon. They were not being fed. And it always seemed to be those men who were the first to get bad attitudes and become hyper-critical. Why? Because they were in the field, but not in the house.

Sometimes I'll hear a comment like this: "Pastor, okay. If I have a choice, I'm not much of a worshipper but I'm more of a worker." I counter with something like, "We need all the workers we can get because there's work to be done. The fields are white in harvest. But if you're sincere about this, I think you first need to get your heart right in worship and get under the Word and get the Word in you. You'll be a much better worker long-term. If you don't do that, you're just going to burn out unless you're doing it just for pride."

How someone reacts to this advice can speak volumes about the heart.

"The older brother became angry and refused to go in. So his father went out and pleaded with him."[45]

The father went out to meet the wayward son on the road. Then, the father had to leave the party and go out to see his older boy. He is a wonderful father. If I'm in a meeting and the Lord is just working: people are being saved, God is just blessing, testifying, we're worshipping God, the Word is being preached, and I get a note, "Mr. So and So is out here in the parking lot and he has a list of grievances. He's not going to come in until you go out and talk to him." I'm probably not going to go out and talk to him.

But the father went out there.

"But he answered his father, 'Look! All these years I've been slaving for you and never disobeyed your orders. Yet you never gave me even a young goat so I could celebrate with my friends.'"[46]

By the way, the older brother was probably also thinking, "You know, you already gave us your inheritance. That calf was mine! I know, Dad, you still think you run things around here." I have a number of friends who have taken over businesses for their father, and one of the funniest things is when the father comes around, people start to look to that guy (he's the boss) and it's really hard sometimes. You can just imagine big brother thinking, "Well, he never asked me about the calf. Oh, and he gave that good-for-nothing rascal a signet ring? He gave him the bank account codes? Seriously?" *"But when this son of yours who has squandered your property with prostitutes comes home, you kill the fattened calf for him!'"*[47] He was angry.

Anger and joy can never occupy the same space.

I was raised in strict fundamentalism. Some of it was good. I got a good, solid, doctrinal grounding. But man, those people were mad all the time at somebody. Their favorite emotion weren't joy or peace, but rather, anger. I actually heard preachers say, "Don't preach unless you're angry about something. If you can't be angry about something, preach against Hershey bars!" I heard a big-name fundamentalist preacher say that. "Just get up and say, 'Those chocolate Hershey bars! They're just of the Devil.'"

The idea seemed to be that you'd be a better preacher when upset or outraged at something. All of us have probably encountered a preacher or two, or a Christian or two, just mad at everything and everybody. I had a guy tell me one time, "You know, Preacher, the strangest thing happened to me in church." He said, "I used to drink a lot and hang out at this particular bar.". He said, "I got saved and I left that kind of life. I started hanging out with Christians and I got to thinking, 'Sometimes those people in that bar treated me better than some of the brothers and sisters in Christ.'"

The older brother was an angry guy. We get angry. Get over it. If you get angry, get over it. But there are people who just love to be angry. They're never happier than when they're unhappy and angry.

The older brother's anger was driven by several things. He felt *superior* to his brother, didn't he? Make a list of how many times tomorrow you criticize something you don't like in someone else. How much of that is driven by the fact you want to feel superior? "Look at that skinny person. They don't even look like they're nourished." Now what am I doing? I'm making myself feel superior because if a famine comes, I'm going to live much longer than they are. Tim Keller, best-selling author and long-time pastor of Redeemer Presbyterian Church in New York City, said this:

"It's impossible to forgive someone if you feel superior to him or her because forgiveness is by its very definition, humility."

Big brother felt superior. He also had feelings of *jealousy*. "You never even gave me a fried chicken, and you made him prime rib! And you took the prime rib from my stock." He was jealous of the party and he was feeling sorry for himself.

One more thing. *Self-righteousness*, which is what this guy was guilty of, the *Big Brother Syndrome*, makes us disrespectful and dismissive. When he talked to his father, do you see what he said? "Look! All these years…" Is that any way to talk to your father? If I ever were to say to my dad when I was younger, "Hey, old man," I would not be an old man today. I'd be dead. Seriously. I didn't talk to him that way. Even when I disagreed with my dad, I didn't talk to him that way. The few times I've been disrespectful have been a terrible thing. The Bible says honor your parents. "Look, old man!" That's basically what he's saying.

He was so disrespectful and unaware of himself. He was so filled with pride. In his self-righteousness, he showed disrespect. He thought his father was weak. He thought his father had been manipulated. He had no respect for the father. Sometimes, when you see God bless somebody and you think they don't deserve it, you think somehow, "Boy, they put one over on God." No. You just don't know God the way you ought to know God.

Then he said, *"This son of yours…"*

When our kids were growing up, if Karen said, "Do you know what your daughter did today?" that was never a good thing. "Do you know what your grandson just did?" You know what she's saying. She's saying all the evil things these kids do and have done comes from the Stokes line of the blood. "I'm a Holland. We're Mary Poppins; practically perfect all the time. Perfect blood. Our blood is blue." "This son of yours…" It's his brother! He wanted to the be the father's *only* son.

Please remember, God has other children.

About every two years, I re-read one of my favorite books, *Mere Christianity* by C.S. Lewis. It's a classic. Every Christian ought to own a copy. It's available everywhere. I've taken Bible studies through it. In Mere Christianity, there is a classic passage:

"The sins of the flesh are bad [like adultery, sexual immorality, drunkenness], but they are the least bad of all sins. All the worst pleasures are purely spiritual: the pleasure of putting other people in the wrong, of bossing and patronising and spoiling sport, and backbiting, the pleasures of power, of hatred. For there are two things inside me, competing with the human self which I must try to become. They are the Animal self [that's the fleshly sins], and the Diabolical self. The Diabolical self is the worse of the two. That is why a cold, self-righteous prig who goes regularly to church may be far nearer to hell than a prostitute. But, of course, it is better to be neither."

I think he hit the nail on the head. Maybe you've never been that prodigal who wandered off. Maybe you've been the brother who stayed home and did it right. You played by the rules—and you're proud of that fact. Don't let it make you feel superior. Don't let that make you feel angry and critical, because that doesn't please God. That's every bit as wicked as the son with the prostitutes and wasting all the money because the Father resists the proud, but gives grace to the humble.

CHAPTER SEVEN

I Am Prodigal

The older brother was angry when he should have been joyful. He missed the whole celebration. Anger is a very, very dangerous thing— especially anger driven by self-righteousness. Certainly, some things should outrage us, but we ought to be very careful about anger that lingers and stays and simmers and seethes.

When my wife and I were first married in the summer of 1976, we were part of a singing group representing our college. We traveled across America with a patriotic musical program for that bicentennial year. On that trip we saw the Pacific, the Atlantic, Canada, and Mexico, and performed in 48 cities. It was a whirlwind tour on a big tour bus with about 25 singers and a few instrumentalists.

This was our honeymoon. We're taking 25 people on our honeymoon with us. There were two married couples who were part of the group. Everybody else was a single college student. When we'd go to a particular town or city, they'd try to put us in a nice place. Because I was going to be a pastor, often we stayed in a local pastor's home.

During that tour, we performed down in Pasadena, Texas, just outside of Houston, and they put us in the home of a pastor. We wound up being there a couple of nights. I don't know how the pastor's wife noticed it, but Karen and I had been bickering a lot. It's a little nerve-racking to be on the road like that. The last morning we were there, she said, "Kids, let me take you out for some breakfast." So she took us to this little place for breakfast. We had coffee, and she said, "I brought you out here to talk to you." She said, "I've noticed that you're a newlywed couple and you've been sort of picking at each other." We were thinking, "Shut up," but she continued on. She finally said, "Let me give you a piece of advice. You need to get over things quickly in your marriage and never, ever go to bed and go to sleep angry. Resolve it that night. The Bible says, 'Let not the sun go down on your wrath.' Resolve things that night."

Best. Advice. Ever.

We've had some arguments over the years. They're never very long, but to this day, after nearly 42 years of marriage, we have never gone to sleep mad at each other. Now, I've had to wake her up a few times to finish the conversation. It's not that we're perfect, but that's a bit of advice we have followed.

Anger is a terrible thing. Some Christians are angry all the time. Did you know the world out there thinks that Christians are a bunch of angry, mean people? We are known more for what we're against than what we're for. I don't think that's the way we ought to be seen. Now if you're going to be *for* Jesus you *are* going to be against certain things Jesus is against, but at the same time let us be primarily known for being for Jesus. I think that's very important.

The prophet Jonah was an angry man. He was petty and prejudiced. Jonah ran from God, and then God rescued him, and then he called him, and Jonah went and preached to the Assyrian city of Nineveh. Then, surprisingly to Jonah, Nineveh repented and had one of the biggest spiritual revivals in human history. But instead of being excited about such a great awakening, Jonah got mad. He wanted the people of Nineveh to experience God's wrath, not God's mercy.

Jonah pouted.

He went out and sat to watch the city, to see what would happen. God grew a big leafy plant to provide shade for the prophet—remember, this was modern day Iraq—a hot place. Jonah was happy about the supernatural vine. In fact, he loved it—he loved it more than he loved anyone in Nineveh. Then a big worm ate the plant, and Jonah was angry again. Then God spoke to Jonah:

"Do you have a right to be angry about the vine?" "I do," he said. "I am angry enough to die." But the Lord said, "You have been concerned about this vine, though you did not tend it or make it grow. It sprang up overnight and died overnight. But Nineveh has more than a hundred and twenty thousand people who cannot tell their right hand from their left, and many cattle as well. Should I not be concerned about great city."[48]

Jonah missed the point.

So did the older brother.

If we're honest, we know that we have the tendencies of both brothers in our story. There's a little propensity in us, under the right circumstances or wrong ones, buttons being pushed, certain things happening, that we could become that Prodigal who quits and runs off. Or we could become the other one who stays home and becomes very angry, negative, cynical, and judgmental. I think we all have both elements. I would also suggest that more church people wrestle with the older brother stuff than the younger brother stuff.

When I was a kid, my pastor father would have preacher friends of his come to preach in our church—sometimes for a week at a time. There was this one preacher who had a fascinating "testimony." He used to be a gangster back in the days of Al Capone, John Dillinger, "Baby Face" Nelson, "Pretty Boy" Floyd, and he wound up going to jail for it. He got saved and became a preacher, and his trademark sermon was to tell his story about being a gangster.

It was a cool story. They had machine guns and fast cars and all kinds of stuff, and then he got saved. When I was a teenager, we'd go to youth rallies and hear former drug addicts share their sensational testimonies. So dramatic.

When God called me to preach, part of me wondered what I would preach—after all, I didn't have a cool story. "Folks, I'll tell you, I started out in a bad place. It was called the church nursery. One day I went to the beginner's department, and then the junior department. Those were all tough transitions. All the gangs in the junior department at church. Tough, tough, tough. Finally, I made it to the youth group."

That was *my* story.

I wasn't doing drugs when I was six years old. I went to church, and then I went to Bible college, and I went into the ministry. I've lived a very good, boring life. I really have. I never messed around with that stuff. So, I can identify with the older brother. And it's easy to look down the nose at someone who has messed up badly.

My mom's younger brother, Barry, was my favorite uncle. He was about 12 or 13 years older than me. He was a bit of clown. He was in trouble a lot. Very James Dean, cool. But the reality was that Barry messed his life up. He was in trouble from the time he was a kid. He messed up big time. He was in trouble with the law. Then he got involved in drugs. I remember they put him in a juvenile home in Lansing, Michigan. It's probably nonexistent now. Very draconian. We have some old home movies of my mother and I visiting there when I was about five years old. I remember seeing him there. I still have the image of seeing my uncle Barry. I later found out that he had been abused in that place, and it hurt him so badly. His life was a mess. He even got married to a wonderful lady, had a wonderful first daughter, and then later other kids, but he was still a mess.

To me, he was cool. He had a big motorcycle and drove a hot rod car, but he was very erratic, always in trouble, couldn't hold a job. He broke my grandparents' heart. My grandfather was something they called a *precision grinder*, sort of a support something for the auto industry, just grinding things. Every time he'd get a bonus he'd have to bail Barry out of jail. He broke my mom's heart, his oldest sister. They prayed for him. We prayed for him.

One day in 1967, when I was eleven years old, I was at church looking out the front doors and saw a loud car pull up under the carport. It was my uncle Barry—and he just parked there. You should have seen some of the ushers. He came in, and of course, I ran and said, "Mom, Uncle Barry is here." She sort of teared up, and then she went to see her mom. "Mama, Barry is here." He came into church that day wearing a green sport jacket, a yellow turtleneck, checkered slacks, alligator shoes, and he wore sunglasses through the whole service, and his hair was all up like an Afro. In that church nobody dressed that way.

Ever.

He got saved that day, got his heart right with God. The next Sunday he got baptized. He was so excited about getting baptized that he started to run down the stairs, and he fell into the water in front of my dad. He cleaned his life up, and he went to work. He was my Sunday school teacher for a while. Lived for the Lord Jesus Christ. I still think about those old guys—the ushers—giving him the eye when he first came in because he looked like he didn't belong there.

That's the spirit of big brother.

The father told his older boy, *"My son, you're always with me. Everything I have is yours."* In other words, "Listen. You've always been here. I get that. I know that." It's like the son was saying, "How come you don't show *me* any attention?"

But the father had been showing it to him all along, and he *did* appreciate it, and God appreciates it.

Here's an important thing to remember: When you're actually doing the job you're supposed to do, you will not get as much attention as the person who's not doing their job.

When you start feeling sorry for yourself, especially in church, you have to ask yourself this question. "Who am I doing this for? What's this about?" If you're serving Jesus and doing it because you want to please the Lord, none of that is going to bother you. But I have to tell you, if you've ever led people, you do appreciate people who are there all the time. Sometimes the screw-up will get more attention, and if it really bothers you, then what's the point? The father said, *"But we had to celebrate and be glad..."* This is required of us. It's part of what we do. *"...because this brother of yours was dead and is alive again; he was lost and is found."*[9]

Why do you think we should be working for the Lord out in "the field?" Why do you think we have the father's house? What's going on in the field? The harvest. And what's the harvest about? Well, the metaphor in Scripture is it's about people. What kind of people? Dead people who are made alive, lost people who are found. We have this constant tension in church life in America, particularly Bible-based churches, trying to balance what church is about.

Is it about evangelism (reaching people, getting people converted) or is it about edification (building people up)? Well, the answer to that question is it is about both. The Great Commission. "Go everywhere, make disciples of all nations," Jesus said, "baptizing them in the name of the Father, the Son, and the Holy Spirit, and then teach them to observe all things."[50]

Every church has to determine its bent, its bias. What's the major? What's the minor? I'll tell you how I've always come down. I've always come down that edification, the building up of the saints, the growing of the already saved, is extremely important, but never at the expense of reaching new people for Jesus, never at the expense of reproduction.

Have you ever heard the story of the Shakers in Upstate New York? They were a group of religiously devout people, and they were really good at making furniture. Sort of like Amish, Mennonite, that kind of thing. There are barely any Shakers left today. One of their laws was they did not believe in sexual relations— even in marriage. They were chaste.

Has anybody figured out why there are no Shakers today?

When you miss the point of reproduction, when you miss the point of seeing other people come to faith, you'll be one generation away from extinction. Yes, I want to edify believers, but I never want to pastor a church (and I do not, by the way) of smug, self-righteous Christians who are only into deeper Bible study and don't really care if the world around them goes to hell.

Why did Jesus come into the world? If he came to build that kind of person, then why wasn't his focus on trying to get the Pharisees to follow him? Because that's what they were about. "We want moral people. We want people who dot their I's and cross their T's like we do." Well, I believe the world is immoral right now. I believe it's darker than it has been in my lifetime. It's almost like the sewage of hell is backing up everywhere.

Morality is out the window. A culture of death, evil. The opiate crisis, flagrant immorality, man's inhumanity to man. It's bad. So what do a lot of Christians do? "Let's just yell at it." Does that help? Guess what? The darker something is, the brighter light will look, and Jesus is the Light of the World. "That's bad news." People think we're just about bad news. No, we're about *good* news. That's the x-ray. We have the cure. It's Jesus Christ and his love. How?

Because he can take something that is dead and make it alive again.

Death in the Bible never speaks of annihilation; it's always about separation of some sort. Paul told the Corinthians, *"Absent from the body, present with the Lord."*[51] I tell people often, "You do not have a soul. You *are* a soul and you *have* a body, because the soul is the real you. It goes on." When you think about this, what is physical death? The soul and the spirit separating from the body. What is spiritual death? Eternal separation from God.

Karen and I like *Masterpiece Theatre*. It's really good. We put the closed captions on, because it's in the English language and we can't understand it. We've been watching this show *Poldark*. Really, really good show. They're in the latter part of the eighteenth century right now. So you have the Church of England, and then you have groups of Methodists who try to come into the churches, and they're all converted drunkards and prostitutes. "They're not like us. They're not holy like us." That's how the Methodist movement started. A century later that's how the Salvation Army started.

All this, against the backdrop of the French Revolution going on over in France in the late 18th century. It was a bloodbath.

Here we had *our* revolution, and we got the Declaration of Independence. We got the Constitution. We've had our mistakes as a culture and we've fixed some of them, but I guarantee you it was never as bad as the French Revolution. They wanted liberty, equality, and fraternity. But it became a bloodbath. It led to the dictatorship of Napoleon, which was the precursor to all political systems of tyranny and totalitarianism to come on the left or the right.

What made the difference between the American Revolution and the French Revolution? We had a spiritual awakening right before our uprising. It doesn't mean they were all saved, but God was sort of tempering the natural power-hungry part of human nature. The French Revolution was decidedly secular, anti-clerical, anti-religion, and it degenerated into a terrible, dystopic bloodbath.[52]

What is hell? Whatever else hell is, it's being separated from life, love, and light for all eternity. Eternal life is being *with* light, love, and life through Jesus Christ for all eternity. "Was dead and is alive; was lost but is now found." Do you know anybody lost in your life, people who just don't know their way?

I heard somebody say one time that every person you know is, a few times in his or her life, at the place where if somebody told them about the love of God they would respond positively. Our job as Christians is to try to keep ourselves near that person for that time. That's powerful, because God is in the business of taking dead things and making them alive, taking lost things and making them found.

My uncle Barry had been lost in a haze of drugs, in a life of rebellion and crime and hurt. He was a victim himself. He was lost, but one day he gave it all to Jesus, and God took it and made it something beautiful, so that that man, who was such a loser, could someday take me and other 12-year-old boys in a Sunday school class and teach us about Jesus.

Yet I still remember those old ushers' faces when he pulled up and parked his car in the wrong place. Are you willing to push through that kind of prejudice to see the real person and the real need? Recently, as I was walking from my office to our church auditorium, a few little children came running around a corner. An adult was trying to catch up. Almost ran me down. The adult said, "Oh, I'm sorry, Pastor." I said, "No problem here."

I told our church the night I was voted in back in 1998, "Rule number one: I don't want to hear anybody talking to kids about behaving themselves in church. I want them here. I want them to think it's Disneyland. We'll take care of that. It'll solve itself." A few smug members were not happy about that. They said things like, "Well, when I was a kid, we were seen and not heard and ignored and unloved." Well, that's why they were like they were. But we don't want children to grow up angry and grumpy. We want them to grow up like happy people.

But, I guess there will always be people who miss the point.

What's the point? Why are we here? What's the *what* and the *why*? Things that are dead need to be alive, things that are lost need to be found, and everything else is subservient to that.

I am prodigal.

So are you.

Whether you're the son who messed up or the son who was full of himself and his own pride, they both needed to come home. The sad thing is we know the younger son came home.

I wonder—did the older brother ever join the party?

EXPECTATION BOOKS

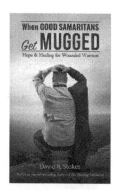

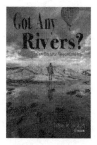

Acknowledgments

A while back, I came across a great quote by Max Lucado that reflected how I feel about the people I get to work with every day. It was in response to a question about how he was able to be so effective as an author, while still a pastor. He said:

"I have a great staff at the church; they protect me and allow me to focus on more of what I do best."

I'm not sure writing is what I do best, but I sure him. I feel the same way about our team.

I want to thank Tracey Dowdy, my editorial assistant. Her early work on this project was essential to what it has become. Also, I am grateful to Rachel Walker for lending her expert eyes to this project. Eowyn Riggins produced yet another great book cover. And Rachel Green at Penn Oaks Publishing has once again produced a great interior layout.

To Karen and our daughters—well, what more can I say? They mean everything to me.

—DRS

About the Author

David R. Stokes is an ordained minister, Wall Street Journal bestselling author, commentator, broadcaster, and columnist. He's been married to the love of his life, Karen, since 1976. They have three daughters and seven grandchildren. And they all live in the great and beautiful Commonwealth of Virginia. He has served as the senior minister at the ministry now known as Expectation Church in Fairfax, Virginia since 1998.

David's website is:
http://www.davidrstokes.com
Follow David on **FACEBOOK**:
https://www.facebook.com/DavidRStokesAuthor/
Follow David on **TWITTER**:
https://twitter.com/DavidRStokes
Follow David on **AMAZON**:
https://amazon.com/author/davidstokes

End Notes

1   Luke 19:10, New International Version
2   Isaiah 53:6, New International Version
3   http://www.christianity.com/church/church-history/timeline/1701-1800/did-
    robert-robinson-wander-as-he-feared-11630313.html
4   Luke 15:1-2, New International Version
5   John 1:12, New International Version
6   See John: 3:1-8, New International Version
7   Luke 15:11-12, New International Version
8   See: *The Story of Lassie: His Discovery and Training from Puppyhood to Stardom*, by Rudd B.
    Rothwell & John H. Weatherwax
9   Hebrews 13:5, New International Version
10 *The Return of the Prodigal Son: A Story of Homecoming*, by Henri J.M. Nouwen,
    Doubleday, New York, p. 43
11 Genesis 13:10, New International Version
12 II Corinthians 11:14, New International Version
13 I Timothy 4:1, King James Version
14 Luke 15:12, New International Version
15 Proverbs 9:10, New International Version
16 Proverbs 19:3, New International Version
17 Luke 15:13, New International Version
18 Genesis 9:20, New International Version
19 From the sermon, "The Prodigal and His Father," Expositions of Holy Scripture, by
    Alexander Maclaren
20 CAL THOMAS COMMENTARY SEPTEMBER 29, 2017
21 Ephesians 5:18, New International Version
22 I Peter 4:3, New International Version
23 Luke 15:14, New International Version
24 Proverbs 29:18, New International Version
25 "The Brothers Karamazov," Fyodor Dostoevsky. Part IV, Book XI, Chapter 73.
26 Psalm 51:12, New International Version
27 I Corinthians 3:10-15, New International Version
28 Revelation 1:14, King James Version
29 Proverbs 22:8, New International Version
30 Will L. Thompson (1847-1909)
31 Luke 15:11-19, New International Version
32 See Acts chapters 6 & 7
33 Acts 9:5, New King James Version
34 Matthew 5:29-30, New International Version
35 II Timothy 1:7, King James Version
36 I Peter 1:13, King James Version
37 Genesis 39:8-12, New International Version

38 Psalm 51:1-3, New International Version
39 Luke 15:18, New International Version
40 See Matthew 5:27-30, New International Version
41 See Matthew 5:27-30, New International Version
42 This section involves Luke 15:21-24, New International Version
43 See Genesis 41:28-42, New International Version
44 Luke 15:25-27, New International Version
45 Luke 15:28, New International Version
46 Luke 15:29, New International Version
47 Luke 15:30, New International Version
48 Jonah 4:9-11, New International Version
49 Luke 15:31-32, New International Version
50 See Matthew 28:19-20, New International Version
51 See II Corinthians 5:8
52 For further reading, see the author's article:
    https://townhall.com/columnists/davidstokes/2014/07/14/the-revolutions-of-july-
    n1861200

61492701R00068

Made in the USA
San Bernardino, CA
15 December 2017